The Islamic Antichrist Myth

I0098310

Why the Beast Is Not
An Arab or a Muslim

Positron Prophecy Series – Book 5

Charles K. Bassett

Positron
Books
Las Vegas, NV

The Islamic Antichrist Myth: Why the Beast Is Not An Arab or a Muslim

Copyright © 2019 by Charles K. Bassett

Published by Positron Books, LLC
Las Vegas, Nevada

First printing: August 2019

ISBN: 978-1-7350402-1-9

Please visit www.Prophecy7000.com [10.8.24] / pb   **Email**: ckbassett777@yahoo.com

Printed in the United States of America

To the Lord Jesus Christ,
God of Heaven and Earth

CONTENTS

* * * The Challenge * * *

If you're reading these words, there's a pretty good chance you support the Islamic Antichrist Theory.

You believe in the so-called 'Mideast Beast.' You believe that the Beast is really the *Mahdi*. You believe he's an Arab who will conquer the world. You have absolutely no doubt he will come out of Syria, Turkey, Iran, Iraq, Egypt, Lebanon, Saudi Arabia, or maybe even Afghanistan.

And above all, you know for a fact he cannot be a Roman Caesar.

So let me ask you something…

Does this make sense?

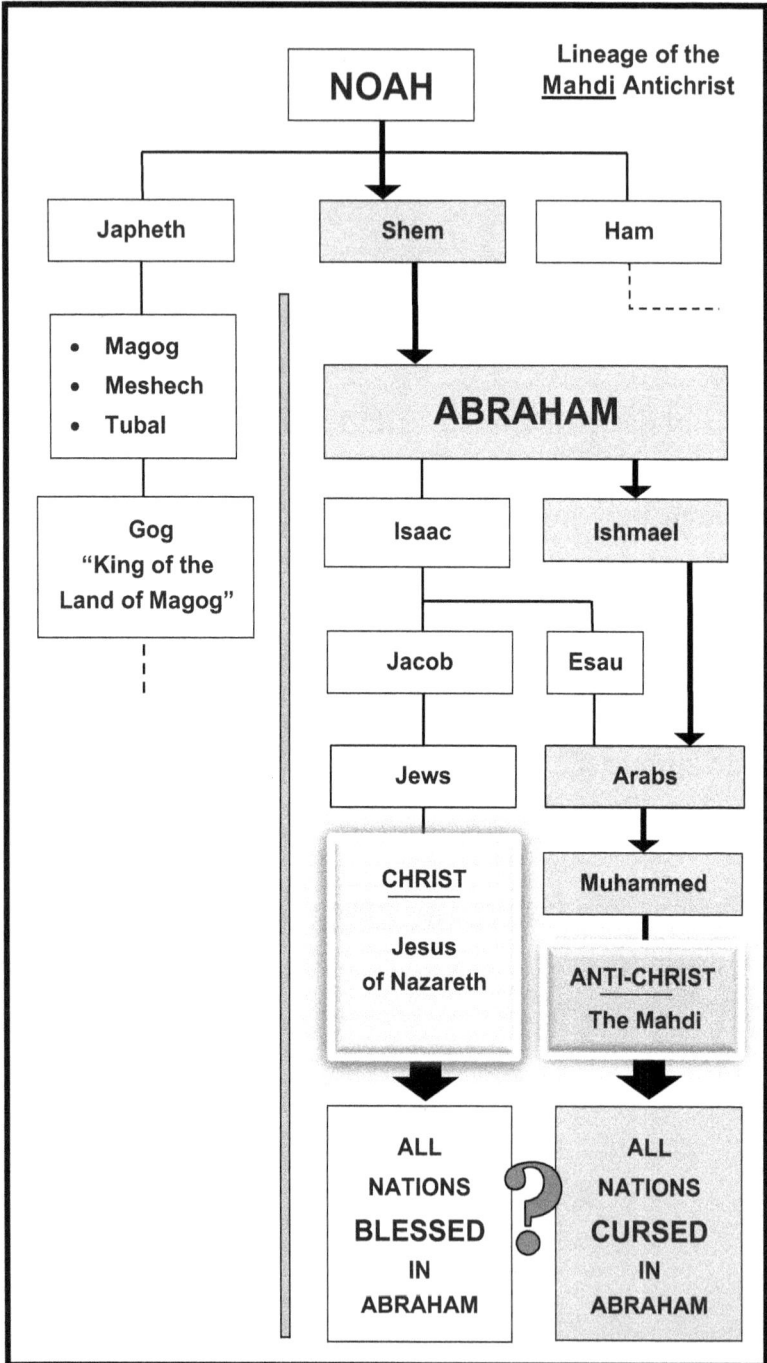

NOAH

Lineage of the <u>Mahdi</u> Antichrist

- Japheth
- Shem
- Ham

Japheth:
- Magog
- Meshech
- Tubal

Gog "King of the Land of Magog"

ABRAHAM

Isaac — Ishmael

Jacob — Esau

Jews — Arabs

CHRIST Jesus of Nazareth

Muhammed

ANTI-CHRIST The Mahdi

ALL NATIONS **BLESSED** IN ABRAHAM

?

ALL NATIONS **CURSED** IN ABRAHAM

...or does this?

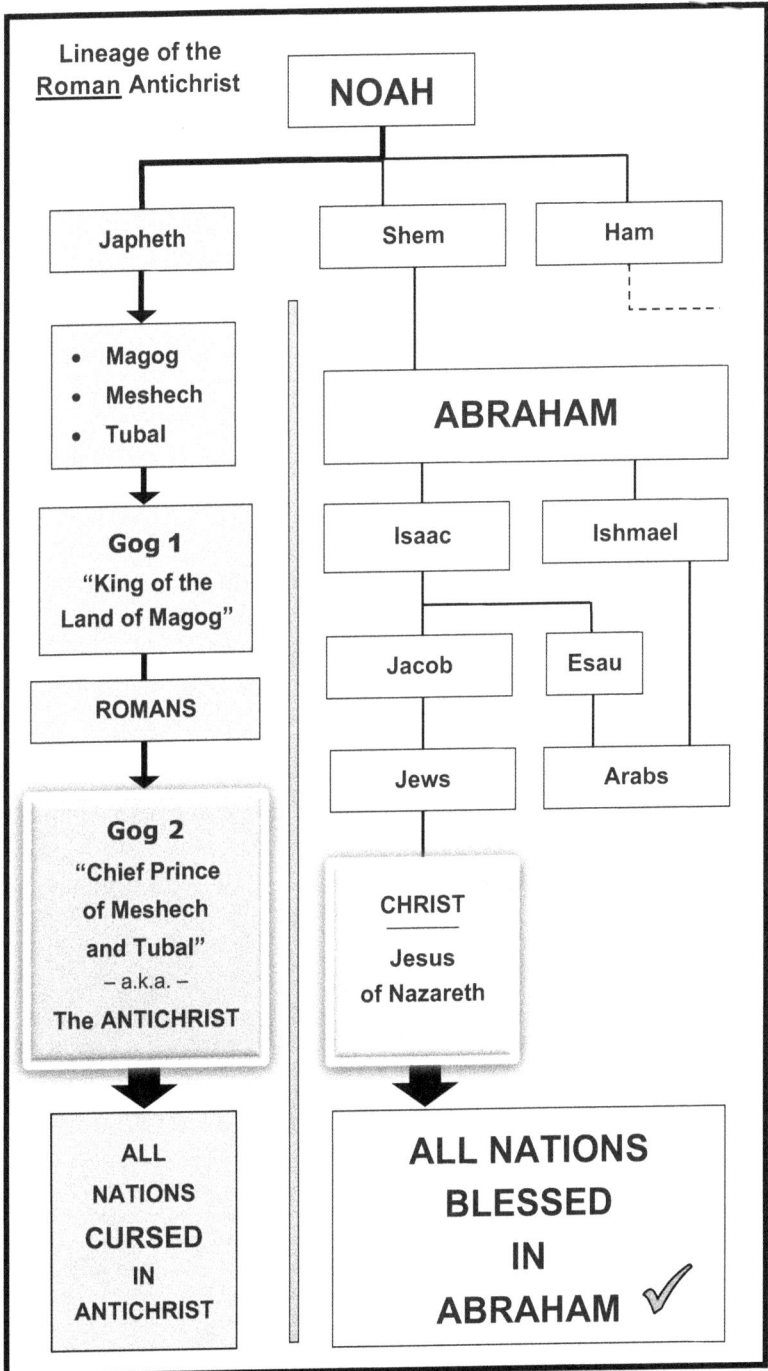

Lineage of the <u>Roman</u> Antichrist

NOAH

- Japheth
- Shem
- Ham

Japheth
- Magog
- Meshech
- Tubal

Gog 1
"King of the Land of Magog"

ROMANS

Gog 2
"Chief Prince of Meshech and Tubal"
– a.k.a. –
The ANTICHRIST

ALL NATIONS CURSED IN ANTICHRIST

ABRAHAM

Isaac

Ishmael

Jacob

Esau

Jews

Arabs

CHRIST
Jesus of Nazareth

ALL NATIONS BLESSED IN ABRAHAM ✓

ABRAHAM'S SEED — A BLESSING OR A CURSE?

Over the past several years, the Islamic Antichrist Theory (IAT) has become the predominant end-times viewpoint of many evangelical Christians. Instead of seeing the Antichrist as a descendant of Rome (as was commonly taught in the 1970s and '80s), they now believe he will descend from Muhammed and rise as the indomitable *Mahdi*, the prophesied savior of Islam.

This change of perspective is troubling because the IAT not only suffers from at least 15 major errors, but it distracts the Church from concentrating on the true point-of-origin of the Antichrist, namely, the nations of Europe, and especially Italy.

However, there is another problem attending the IAT which is so egregious that I feel compelled to address it right here. Simply stated:

> **If the Mahdi of Islam is the biblical Antichrist — as IAT backers insist — then God's solemn promise to** *bless* **the nations through** *Abraham* **(Gen. 22:18) was a colossal sham.**

Why? Because according to virtually every Muslim scholar, any man who claims to be the Mahdi *must first be* an Arab.[1] And Arabs are descended from **Abraham**,[2] the man who is supposed to *bless* all nations by producing Jesus Christ (Gen. 22:18), not *curse* all nations by producing the Antichrist.

---

[1] Muslims will not accept anyone as the Mahdi unless that person has Arabic roots. This is because almost every hadith concerning the subject says the Mahdi will descend from the line of Muhammed—and Muhammed was Arabic. See *The Islamic Antichrist,* by Joel Richardson (p. 23 and 31). Also see the Wikipedia articles: "Mahdi" and "Twelver Shi'ism." Also see ▶ thepromisedmahdi.com/sunni-documentation-on-mahdi-as

[2] According to Wikipedia ["Arabs"]: "Both Judaism and Islam see Ishmael [and thus, Abraham] as the ancestor of the Arabic people. Ishmael is recognized by Muslims as the ancestor of several prominent Arab tribes... Muslims also believe that Muhammad was the descendant of Ishmael... Assyrians referred to the Arab tribes as Ishmaelites, or "Shu-mu'ilu" as recorded in their inscriptions... [And] the tribes of Central West Arabia called themselves the 'people of Abraham and the offspring of Ishmael.'"

Or to say it another way, if the Islamic Antichrist Theory is true, then those who support it somehow believe it is possible for all nations to be *blessed in Abraham* through Jesus of Nazareth, yet *cursed in Abraham* through the Mahdi of Islam — at the same time!

Unless I'm missing something, I would say that's an extremely untenable position. Are we really supposed to believe that righteous Abraham is the progenitor of both God's Son and Lucifer's hellion?

Even Matthew and James say (in effect) it is impossible for Salvation and Damnation to flow from the same source:

> **Matthew 7:17, 20** (NIV) — Likewise, every good tree bears good fruit, but a bad tree bears bad fruit... Thus, by their fruit you will recognize them.

> **James 3:11-12** (NIV) — Can both fresh water and salt water flow from the same spring? My brothers and sisters, can a fig tree bear olives, or a grapevine bear figs? Neither can a salt spring produce fresh water.

Consequently, there is only one possible conclusion regarding the Antichrist's lineage: he *has to* emerge from a line *other than* Abraham's. Which means the Antichrist cannot be an Arab. Which means he cannot be the Mahdi. Which means the IAT theory is void on its face.

[In fact, I believe that Ezekiel 38:2-3 tells us the Antichrist will come from the line of Japheth, and his sons Magog, Meshech, and Tubal. Please see Appendix D for a full discussion.]

In the meantime, having covered what is perhaps the most illogical aspect of the Islamic Antichrist Theory, the rest of this book will now address 15 popular arguments which are used to support the IAT and explain why each are mistaken. Specifically, I will explain why:

1. The "people" whom Daniel (predictively) blamed for the 70 A.D. destruction of Jerusalem and the Temple were *not* the Arabs.

2. Satan's capital is *not* located in Pergamum (a city in Turkey).

3. The "king of the north" does *not* have to be Middle Eastern.

4. The absence of the word "Rome" in prophecy proves *nothing*.

5. Revelation's composite beast is *not* a "composite Arab."

6. Antiochus IV is *not* Daniel's "king of fierce countenance."

7. Muslims will *not* accept any "Mahdi" who claims to be God.

8. Mecca is *not* Mystery Babylon. (Neither is Saudi Arabia.)

9. Prophecy does *not* say the 4th Empire absorbs the first three.

10. The simultaneous collapse of all four empires does *not* mean they are joined under the Antichrist.

11. Islamic prophecy *cannot* be used to glean any knowledge concerning the Beast.

12. The various Antichrist forerunners (in most cases) do *not* reflect his nationality.

13. The Antichrist will *not* refrain from claiming to be "God."

14. The Antichrist is *not* the leader of Muslims at Armageddon.

15. The Greeks and Persians of Daniel 8 are *not* modern empires.

Sound interesting? Then let us begin…

Chapter 1

A POPULAR THEORY

ATTENTION EVERYONE: IT'S OFFICIAL! Over a dozen of the most celebrated pastors and authors have finally rejected the idea of a *European Antichrist*, and have now embraced the notion of a *Muslim Antichrist*. This dramatic shift has taken almost twenty years to accomplish, and the transformation has proceeded in fits and starts. But the shift can no longer be denied, and many of the Christian leaders who hold this position are now going all-out to prove it.[3]

The Antichrist?

According to the interpretation held by these good men and women, the Bible's "Man of Sin" will not be a Roman, as was previously thought. Instead, he will be a militant Muslim. He will rise to power somewhere in the Middle East. He will be embraced by his kinsmen as the long-awaited *Mahdi* (savior of Islam). And his armies will fight against Christ at the Battle of Armageddon.

---

[3] See Appendix B for a short list of Evangelicals who say the Antichrist will be a Muslim.

To be sure, this position — known as the Islamic Antichrist Theory — is relatively new. It began about twenty years ago, shortly after a handful of vicious Islamic terrorists flew two airliners into the Twin Towers in lower Manhattan, killing almost 3000 Americans. But the recency of this theory hasn't stopped it from taking a large section of the Evangelical community by storm. Indeed, many preachers now openly view the Beast of Revelation and the Whore of Babylon through the eyes of Muslim eschatology. Entire congregations are now convinced the Antichrist will be a Muslim because, among other things, the religion of Islam explicitly demands the decapitation of those who reject their faith, a form of punishment that is eerily similar to the one mentioned in Revelation 20.

As a result of these developments, the sale of books and videos extolling (or at least discussing) the Islamic Antichrist Theory (IAT) is at an all-time high. Titles such as *Bad Moon Rising* and *The Assyrian Antichrist* fill the shelves of popular bookstores, while others, such as *The Islamic Antichrist,* by Joel Richardson, have reached the New York Times Bestseller list. Prophecy conferences across the nation now feature experts who are sure the Antichrist will come out of Turkey, Jordan, or Syria. And more than a few websites have appeared, dedicated to promoting this new "Mideast Beast" scenario. Meanwhile, the traditional view of the Antichrist, which holds that the Man of Sin will come out of Europe and descend from the Roman Empire, is quickly being discarded.

The question is, after teaching for decades that the Antichrist will rise from the European continent as the final "Caesar" of planet earth, why are pastors and commentators now jettisoning that position so rapidly? Why are so many Christians abandoning the idea of a Roman Antichrist and flocking to that of an Islamic Mahdi?

Given the current international landscape, the answer isn't that difficult...

ISLAM ASCENDANT

In the first place, despite all the convincing sermons and articles that were produced in the 1970s and '80s claiming that the Beast of the Apocalypse would rise in Europe and descend from the Roman Empire, there doesn't seem to be any indication that particular scenario is about to unfold. At least, not in the immediate future. Nothing in the realm of European politics, commerce, or religion seems to suggest that the Antichrist is about to make his grand debut in Britain, France, Italy, or any other EU (European Union) country. The Christian community has thus been forced to look elsewhere for Satan's ambassador. And the most logical place seems to be the people and nations of Islam.

You see, in agreement with prophecies such as Psalm 83 — which predict that Israel's neighbors will conspire to destroy her in the last days — dozens of Arabic groups have been warring against the Jewish homeland for the last seventy years. And they're only getting more bold. Their latest track record includes two uprisings in the West Bank and Gaza (1987, 2000), forty-two Scud missile attacks during the Gulf War (1991), three devastating conflicts in Lebanon (1982, 1985, 2006), and three more in Gaza (2008, 2012, 2014).

Moreover, in agreement with prophecies such as John 16:2 and Isaiah 59:6 — which predict that horrific massacres will be carried out in the end times by people who claim to be serving God — Islamic terrorists continue to ruthlessly maim and slaughter people all over the planet. The atrocities committed in New York (2001), Bali (2002), Madrid (2004), London (2005), Mumbai (2008), Nigeria (2011), Boston (2013), and Paris (2015) are but a few of the most recent. Sadly, the rate and scope of these attacks are only increasing.

Little wonder, then, that the Islamic Antichrist Theory has gained so much traction. The spike in Arab violence that is occurring all over the world, combined with the unmistakable decline in European power, only makes it appear more likely that the ultimate nemesis of Israel and Christendom will come out of the Islamic nations, not Europe or Rome. At least, that's how it looks right now.

So how should we interpret all of this? How should Christians respond to the Islamic Antichrist Theory, given all the above facts?

HOLD FAST TO THE TRUTH

While it might be tempting to join the IAT crowd and start chasing the "Islamic Antichrist" bandwagon, especially when that hypothesis has the backing of so many prominent Christians, we cannot allow today's Middle East headlines or even the apparent absence of a Roman Antichrist to drive our understanding of God's Word. To do so would be to substitute solid analysis for "newspaper exegesis." We would be drawing conclusions based on current events, rather than on what the Bible actually says.

I'll grant that those who support the Islamic Antichrist Theory are some of the most articulate and well-respected leaders in the Christian community. They know their Bible and they have a solid handle on the relevant prophecies and secular history.

I will also concede that the notion of a Muslim Antichrist has surpassed the Roman Antichrist position among a large number of Evangelicals. Given the earlier success of such well-known authors as Hal Lindsey and Jack Van Impe, both of whom taught that the Antichrist would come out of Europe, that's quite a feat. It speaks to the persuasiveness of the IAT arguments.

Nevertheless, the main question for any new doctrine or position is not whether that doctrine or position is popular, but whether it aligns with the Word of God. We cannot allow the popularity of a given theory to override what God has already said, even when that theory seems to be supported by current events.

Therefore, the validity of the Islamic Antichrist position comes down to one question: Do the prophecies that speak of the Antichrist point to an Islamic Mahdi, or to a Roman Caesar? When the Bible addresses the identity of the Antichrist *specifically*, does it say that the Beast will emerge from an empire that didn't exist until 600 years after Christ left this earth, or does it say that the Antichrist will descend from the empire that subjugated Judaea, leveled Jerusalem, obliterated the Temple, slaughtered a million Jews, exiled the rest, and crucified the very apple of God's eye, Jesus of Nazareth?

Unfortunately, and despite my genuine respect for those who say otherwise, I believe the answer must be the latter. The Bible teaches that the Beast will come out of Rome. That is the consistent testimony of Scripture whenever it touches the subject of Antichrist. And that means the Islamic Antichrist Theory cannot be true.

ERROR UPON ERROR

The attempt to make the Islamic Antichrist Theory fit Bible prophecy has led to a number of unforced errors. If you've studied this theory at all, then it's likely you've already come across some of these miscalculations. The list includes such basic mistakes as:

- Claiming that the "green" horse of Revelation 6:8 signals the green flag of Islam, even though no flag is mentioned in the passage, and despite the fact that "chloros," the relevant Greek word, can also mean *gray* or *ashen* (as in rotting flesh),[4] and is translated in almost every English Bible (here in verse 8) not as "green," but as pale, gray, pallid, sickly green, or ashen.

- Citing the practice of using a clay headrest at prayer time (by some Muslims), as evidence that Islam is the empire of "iron and clay" mentioned in Daniel 2.

- Claiming that the Greek letters for 666 (χξς) are actually Arabic pictograms for "In the name of Allah we will make war," even though Arabic *didn't exist* when Revelation was written, and despite the fact that today's Arabic symbols do not actually match the letters.[5]

---

[4] See, for example ▶ brandplucked.webs.com/rev68apalehorse.htm

[5] See, for example ▶ https://eutychusnerd.blogspot.com/2010/07/the-mark-of-beast-is-islam-walid.html

- Shaming American Christians for "failing" to see that prophecy is Middle East-centered, and that the Antichrist must therefore be Middle Eastern or Arabic, even though Israel's worst enemy, the Roman Empire, came out of Europe.

- Relying on a contrived pun in Daniel 2:43 ("mixed" = *ereb* [Heb.] = *Arab*) to detect the ethnicity of the final empire ("iron mixed with clay.")

- Claiming that the method of execution mentioned in Revelation 20:4 — decapitation — points directly at Islam, despite the fact that beheadings have been used by societies throughout history, including Europe, as late as 1977.

- Claiming that the Seventh Head of the Beast — the only one forecast to reign but a "*short time*" (Rev. 17:10) — is the Islamic Caliphate, even though the Caliphate lasted longer than the empires of Babylon, Medo-Persia, and Greece *put together*.

- Claiming that only a Muslim would deny the full sonship and/or divinity of Jesus (in accordance with 1 John 2:22), even though Mormons, Buddhists, Hindus, Sikhs, Jews, atheists, deists, and Watch Tower members *do exactly the same*, and even though Catholics are *also* known to pick-and-choose which doctrines they will reject or accept (such as Catholic politicians, who openly support *Roe v. Wade* and killing unborn babies; and Pope Francis, who insists that all "good" people will get into heaven, whether or not their faith is in Christ.)

To be fair, not every expositor who supports the Islamic Antichrist Theory makes the above mistakes. But several of these good men and women come dangerously close to doing so, or to relying on Islamic teachings to validate their position. Some even go so far as to say that the parallels between the Bible and Islamic prophecies are "amazing" or "startling," which suggests (whether intended or not) that Islamic prophecy somehow reinforces the prophecies of the Bible!

WHY ISLAMIC PROPHECY CANNOT REVEAL THE IDENTITY OF THE ANTICHRIST

The one thing we must remember throughout this discussion is this: Islamic end-time traditions do not come from the Holy Spirit. They come from a number of Muslim clerics who took fragments of the Old and New Testament (and other sources) to produce their own doomsday scenario. As a result, Muslim eschatology is completely unreliable for our purposes, and even within the Muslim community it is often inconsistent and sketchy. (For example, one tradition holds that their messiah, the Mahdi, has been living in a cave since the Tenth Century, while another says he is yet to be born.)

Allow me to expand: Islamic prophecy is not inspired by the Spirit of Christ. It therefore cannot be used to analyze, verify, support, corroborate, or inform our interpretation of any passage or concept in Scripture regarding the Antichrist or the end times. It can only be used to explain why Muslims might embrace the Beast as an ally, or perhaps receive him (at first) as a wise and exalted teacher. But Islamic texts cannot be used to validate, source, determine, or deduce the Antichrist's religion, career, nationality, ethnic background, or any other characteristic.

Instead, the only writings capable of giving us that information and predicting the future are contained in the Bible (Isaiah 46:9-10). And that is the only source to which we should look.

If we do that — if we look exclusively to God's Word, and allow it to drive our understanding of the Antichrist and current events — we will find that the Bible clearly reveals the Antichrist's nationality, empire, physical appearance, personality, and even his religion. And none of these have anything to do with Islam.

* * * *

Note – You will occasionally see a rule notation at the end of a sentence, such as "(Rule 2)." This indicates that the sentence or statement is based on one of my *Rules of Interpretation* (located in the Appendix), and the rule should be reviewed in order to grasp why that particular statement is legitimate. There are just ten rules and I believe you will find them to be both intriguing and enlightening.

Chapter 2

WHAT THEY'RE SAYING

AS WE LEARNED in the previous chapter, the Islamic Antichrist Theory is one of the most intriguing conjectures ever to hit the modern end-times debate. In fact, it has gained quite a significant following over the past few years, and it's not hard to see why. The Middle East remains a political powder keg, Islamic terrorists continue to maim and kill people all over the planet, and it seems that a Roman Antichrist is never going to come out of Europe.

Further, the Islamic Antichrist Theory has been promoted by many respectable writers and preachers, and each has produced some fairly convincing arguments in support of their position. These good brethren are sincere and intelligent, and they genuinely care about leading others to Christ. While I disagree with their conclusions about the Man of Sin, I have no doubt that their attempt to correlate today's political realities with Bible prophecy is born out of a genuine desire to understand God's Word and to see people saved. Each of these expositors has added to the discussion of eschatology and is worthy of our love and respect.

I would therefore like to continue that discussion by quoting, with courtesy, some of these speakers and authors, so that all of us can understand exactly what they're saying. Afterwards, I'll present my reasons for drawing a different conclusion.

JOHN MACARTHUR

> Let me summarize [what Muslims believe about the Mahdi.] The Mahdi will be a messianic figure... He will be an unparalleled, unequalled leader. He will come out

of a crisis of turmoil. He will take control of the world. He will establish a new world order. He will destroy all who resist him. He will invade many nations. He will make a seven-year peace treaty with the Jews. He will conquer Israel and massacre the Jews. He will establish Islamic world headquarters at Jerusalem. He will rule for seven years [and] establish Islam as the only religion. He will come on a white horse with supernatural power. He will be loved by all people on earth.

If that sounds familiar, that is a precise description of the biblical Antichrist. Absolutely step-by-step-by-step-by-step. The Bible's Antichrist is their Mahdi...

Why am I giving you all this? Because the description of the Mahdi is exactly the description of the biblical Antichrist, the Beast of Revelation 13. And you go into any kind of a study of that, and you will find that all the details match up perfectly.[6]

Pastor MacArthur is an incredibly gifted teacher and a dedicated shepherd of God's people. He deserves a "double portion" of honor in recognition of his lifelong work to guide, teach, and strengthen the Body of Christ. However, as a result of the above sermon, thousands of Christians now believe the Antichrist must be the Mahdi of Islam because MacArthur implies that the teachings of Islam somehow reinforce Bible prophecy: "[T]he description of the Mahdi is exactly the description of the biblical Antichrist." While I'm certain that MacArthur places no stock in the prophecies of Islam, it is clear that, at the very least, he *does* believe the Antichrist will be a Muslim, because after mentioning the above similarities, he then announces that, based on Ezekiel 38 and Revelation 17, the Antichrist will emerge from the eastern half of the old Roman Empire, an area that is almost completely dominated by Islam today. And that means, according to MacArthur, the Islamic nations listed in Ezekiel 38 — not the nations of Europe — will form his power-base.[7]

---

[6] https://m.youtube.com/watch?v=b-f8zDeqy-k [11:45–13:10] "The Mahdi is the AntiChrist" – Pastor John MacArthur. Published 12/12/2017.

[7] Please see Appendix C for a transcript of Pastor MacArthur's statement on this issue.

Soon their savior [the savior of Europe] will appear. It will be the Antichrist, [the man] who's going to introduce to Europe and to the world a one-world currency, a one-world government, and a one-world religion…

So we're talking now about a worldwide religion [under the Antichrist]. I believe that's going to be Islam. It already exists…

The question is—and I've been asked this a number of times in the past few months—*Is the Antichrist in the Bible and the Mahdi of Islam the same person?*

So let's compare the Bible and its description of the Antichrist, and the Koran of the Mahdi, who is the Islamic messiah:

One, the Islamic messiah will be a powerful, political, military, world leader. In the Bible…the Antichrist is exactly the same.

Secondly, the Islamic messiah will be a spiritual world leader and will cause anyone who practices any other religion, other than Islam, to renounce that faith and worship Islam, or be beheaded (you see that with ISIS now)… The Antichrist is a spiritual world leader who will demand that the world worship him. Those who do not will be beheaded…

Thirdly, the Antichrist will target Christians and Jews for death… The Islamic messiah will target Christians and Jews for death.

Four, the Antichrist will set up his image on the Temple Mount in Jerusalem for the world to worship him and call him "God"… The Islamic messiah will attack Jerusalem and try to conquer it for Islam, in order to establish an Islamic rule over the earth and to rule with Islamic law, Shariah law, from the city of Jerusalem.

Five, the Antichrist will offer Israel a seven-year treaty... The Islamic messiah wil offer exactly the same.

Six, the Antichrist comes riding on a white horse... The Islamic messiah comes riding on a white horse, in the Koran.

Seven, the Antichrist will set times and change laws... The Islamic messiah, with Shariah law all over the earth, will set times and change laws.

Seven out of seven—not bad! If it was one, that's a coincidence. If it was two, that would concern you. But when you have seven exact comparisons, *I think you can say that they are one-and-the-same person.*[8]

Pastor Hagee is an outstanding preacher and expositor of the Word. I have personally been blessed by his powerful and uplifting sermons. He is worthy of our deepest respect and admiration. Yet, as with Pastor MacArthur, I believe his analysis concerning the "Muslim Antichrist" is totally incorrect. Why? Because it assumes that Islamic prophecy is reliable (it matches "seven out of seven" biblical prophecies), and it can therefore be used to corroborate the Antichrist's religion and nationality.

According to Pastor Hagee, the Antichrist will not be a Roman Caesar, but a Muslim leader — the *Mahdi* — who will emerge from the territory of the old Roman Empire, and then galvanize a vicious coalition of Middle East nations at the time of the end.

JOEL RICHARDSON

Joel Richardson is an exceptional speaker and writer. He is also the most well-known proponent of the Islamic Antichrist Theory.

---

[8] https://www.youtube.com/watch?v=y0utkD3gjtc [14:26—14:40 and 20:12—23:00] "John Hagee 2016, The King of the West The Final Game of Thrones March 13, 2016"

To his credit, Richardson recognizes the fallacy of using Islamic prophecy to prove the Antichrist will be a Muslim, and he therefore avoids employing Islamic oracles to support his conclusions:

> I am in complete agreement…regarding the fact that many of the Islamic narratives are merely borrowed and distorted versions of Biblical, Gnostic and Zoroastrian accounts... My research simply shows what the ancient Islamic tradition has led Muslims to expect.[9]

> And I would never look to Islamic prophecy as if it is actually prophetic. Muslim apocalyptic material is worth understanding only to see that Satan has been working to create a counter narrative for those who are deceived. But I do not look to it as any source of truth.[10]

In accordance with these statements, Richardson wisely avoids the trap of conferring legitimacy on Islamic writings. Instead, he bases his view of the Islamic Antichrist on a comprehensive analysis of the relevant scriptures in God's Word. Moreover, he patiently reminds his audience that he's not dogmatic about his conclusions. "The future could throw us a *curve ball*," he often quips.

For these reasons, I sincerely value and respect Joel Richardson. I believe his books and YouTube videos have been a big "plus" for the end-times debate. He has provided the Church with a great deal of insight regarding end-times prophecy and he's given us a lot of food for thought. I genuinely commend him.

Still, I must disagree with my brother's assessment regarding the Antichrist's origin, namely, that he'll rise in the Middle East as the Mahdi of Islam. Why? Because his analysis of the Bible, in my opinion, contains numerous errors in logic. Here are just a few that appear in *Mideast Beast* (paraphrased):

---

[9] https://joelstrumpet.com/wp-content/uploads/2014/12/A_Response_to_Dr_Reagans_Article-Will_the_Antichrist_be_a_Muslim-Joel_Richardson.pdf (p. 7)

[10] https://joelstrumpet.com/?p=5731 (Richardson's response to a blog question.)

- **Hasty Generalization** – *The Antichrist must be an Arab, because the Bible repeatedly says that Arabic nations are going to be destroyed at Armageddon, the same battle where the Antichrist will be destroyed* (*Mideast Beast*, p. 5, 36-37).

  It is true that, in connection with Armageddon, the Bible often emphasizes the punishment of Arabic nations like Edom, Moab, and Egypt. But that doesn't permit us to generalize and say that the Antichrist must therefore be an Arab. The Bible also says that many *non-Arabic* nations are going to be punished at the same place and time (Rev. 16:14), and the Antichrist could just as easily come from one of them.

- **Argument from Silence** – *The Antichrist cannot be a Roman or a European, because the Bible never explicitly names "Rome" or "Europe" in connection with end-time prophecy* (*Mideast Beast*, p. 36).

  The mere fact that Scripture doesn't outright name "Europe" or "Rome" in connection with end-time prophecy doesn't mean the Antichrist cannot come from that part of the world, or that Scripture doesn't point to that area by some other means, such as by compass direction, specified actions, timing markers, royal lineage, divine retribution, etc. (Please see IAT Claim #4, plus chapter 5 of this book.)

- **Argument from Fallacy** – *The Antichrist must be from an Arabic country because my opponents are wrong when they say those countries are mere 'allegory' in connection with end-time prophecy* (*Mideast Beast*, p. 18-20, 23, 39).

  Richardson is correct that his opponents are in error—the countries mentioned by his opponents (Moab, Edom, Seir, Amalek) are *not* mere allegory in Numbers 24, Isaiah 25, and so on. But that doesn't automatically mean the Antichrist must be an Arab. Remember, just because one viewpoint is wrong, doesn't mean the opposing viewpoint is right.

- **Single Cause Fallacy** – *The Antichrist must be an Arab because Jesus will judge the nations that divided Israel, and Scripture only blames Arabic nations for dividing Israel* (*Mideast Beast*, p. 33).

  The Bible indeed says that Arabic nations will cause Israel to be divided. This will almost certainly happen through the treaty of Daniel 9:27, which will be negotiated by the Antichrist. But the Bible does *not* say that Arabs will be the only cause of that division, or that no other factions will be involved in the division of Israel. Richardson himself observes that several American pastors are now calling for such a division, and nothing in Scripture excludes a European Antichrist from helping to divide Israel, as well.

- **Changing the Rules** – *The Antichrist's kingdom must be near the ancient city of Babylon, because King Nebuchadnezzar's foreboding dream pivots on what will happen to the Kingdom of Babylon* (*Mideast Beast*, p. 71-72).

  After going to great lengths to prove that *prophecy pivots on Israel,* Richardson suddenly switches that axiom to *prophecy pivots on Babylon,* in order to accommodate the Islamic Antichrist Theory. One cannot change the method of interpreting Scripture in midstream and expect to remain credible.

- **Misquoting Scripture** – *Daniel said that the final empire would possess and occupy the territory of all the previous empires, i.e., the territories of Babylon, Medo-Persia, and Greece. According to Daniel 2:40 (NKJV): "[The final empire] will break in pieces and crush <u>all the others</u>." This is a major detail that was fulfilled by the Islamic Caliphate, but not by Rome* (*Mideast Beast*, p. 63-64).

  In stark contrast to the NKJV Bible cited by Richardson, the original manuscript of Daniel 2:40 does not include the last three words "all the others." It therefore does not say what Richardson claims. (One can easily verify this discrepancy by simply reviewing the KJV, KJ3, and YLT, along with every available interlinear Bible.) Citing Bible versions that fundamentally alter the meaning of the text, especiallly when that text is being used to make one's case, is not an acceptable method of exegesis (to say the least).

I salute Joel Richardson for his dedication to the study of end-time events and for refusing to attach any credibility to Islamic prophecy. His grasp of history is solid and he has an exceptional gift for writing. However, as you can see from the above examples, his analysis of Scripture is marred by faulty reasoning and/or fluctuating ground rules *at almost every critical juncture.*

Consequently, Richardson's conclusions, along with those of Pastors Hagee and MacArthur, cannot be relied upon. Instead, they are fundamentally flawed and should be set aside.

Indeed, the Islamic Antichrist Theory, in my view, is dead-on-arrival. All that remains is to turn on the lamp and examine the corpse. And we can do that by simply reviewing fifteen major errors which are made by those who support it.

Chapter 3

15 ERRORS IN THE
ISLAMIC ANTICHRIST THEORY

THE FOLLOWING SECTION covers fifteen specific errors that are often made by those who support the Islamic Antichrist Theory.

There's a fair amount of material to review, but for those who enjoy the study of eschatology it should prove to be both intriguing and enjoyable. Moreover, I've placed each argument into the following format to make the whole section easier to read:

1) A brief **statement** of the claim

2) A synopsis of the **support** for each claim

3) An explanation of **why the claim is false**

Once all fifteen errors are taken into account, the Islamic Antichrist Theory collapses under its own weight, and no option remains but to realize that the Antichrist cannot be a Muslim. Instead, he must be an Italian who will lead a revived Roman Empire from Europe.

Let's begin…

IAT CLAIM #1 – The Antichrist will come from the Arabic race because those are the "people" who tore down the Temple in 70 A.D.

<u>SUPPORT</u>: Almost 700 years prior to the event, Daniel the prophet predicted that the Temple in Jerusalem would be demolished by an

unspecified group of "people...that shall come" (Dan. 9:26). According to those who support the Islamic Antichrist Theory, the "people who came" were the progenitors of the Arabic nations, specifically, the Middle East tribesmen who had joined the Roman army as auxiliaries:

> **Daniel 9:26** – And after threescore and two weeks shall Messiah [Jesus] be cut off, but not for himself: and the **people of the prince** that shall come **shall destroy the city** [Jerusalem] and the **sanctuary** [the Temple]; and the end thereof shall be with a flood, and unto the end of the war desolations are determined.

Most conservative scholars agree this is a description of the horrific destruction of Jerusalem and the Temple which had been ordered by Nero in the First Century A.D.

However, while the Romans might have been in charge of the Temple's destruction in 70 A.D., the "people" who physically carried out that destruction were conscripts taken from the local tribes: Syrians, Ammonites, Edomites, Egyptians, and other Middle Eastern groups. These "locals" made up about 80% of the Roman forces in Judaea, and their descendants became today's Arabic nations.

Thus, Daniel's prediction that the Antichrist (the "prince") belongs to the "people...that shall come" means he will come from an Arabic nation.

WHY THIS ARGUMENT IS FALSE: The armies of virtually every ancient empire included both homegrown troops *and* foreign auxiliaries. That in itself was nothing unusual. History informs us that the ranks of the foreign units (in just about every major army) were typically filled by soldiers who were either pressed into service after being conquered, or who voluntarily came from afar to join the army as mercenaries.

Yet, God never considered the nationality of the hired help to determine which "people" were responsible for attacking Israel, and therefore which should be punished. It was always the people in command who were held accountable, not the foreign auxiliaries. It was the nationality of the emperor and his senior officers that determined which "people" were to blame, and thus, which ones were under God's condemnation. Consider these examples:

1491 B.C. – Egypt threatens to annihilate the Hebrew slaves.
Punishment: All the firstborn of *Egypt* slaughtered in one night (Ex. 12:29-30). *Pharaoh* and his entire chariot force drowned in the Red Sea (Ex. 14:26-30). No mention of foreign auxiliaries.

701 B.C. – Assyria threatens to destroy Jerusalem.
Punishment: The entire camp of 185,000 *Assyrians* killed in one night. *King Sennacherib* assassinated by his own sons twenty years later (2 Kings 19:35-37). No mention of foreign auxiliaries.

607 B.C. – Babylon crushes the Jews and raids the Temple.
Punishment: The entire empire of *Babylon* subjugated in one night. *King Belshazzar* killed at a banquet (Dan. 5). No mention of foreign auxiliaries.

In all the above instances, there is no record of God singling out the foreign soldiers of any of those armies, and then claiming that their countries (much less their descendants) were to blame for the empire's transgressions. *This is true regardless of the degree to which those auxiliaries participated in the offense.* Instead, it was always the nation of the man in charge — the one who made the decision to go to war — that was identified and summarily punished by the Lord.

Likewise, the same holds true for the destruction of Jerusalem in 70 A.D.: Syrian conscripts might have participated in physically tearing down the Temple, but the "people" who bear the responsibility for that destruction were the Romans, because they were the "people" in charge. They were the ones running the show.

The facts of history conclusively prove this. In the first place, it was two Italian generals (Vespasian and Titus), acting under the authority of an Italian emperor (Nero), who ordered four legions to surround the city and the Temple. Next, it was an Italian officer corps which carried out the ensuing operation for three and a half years. After that, it was an Italian honor guard that raised Caesar's banners over the Temple mount and proclaimed the Italians' victory. After that, it was the legions of Rome — Macedonica, Fretensis, Fulminata, and Apollinaris — which forced the surviving population to flee the country. And finally, it was an Italian capital — Rome — to which the Temple treasures and defeated Jewish commanders were taken.[11]

In short, it was not the war machine of any Middle East chieftain that perpetrated the horrific bloodbath in First Century Israel. It was the war machine of three of the most scandalous Italians in history: Nero, Vespasian, and Titus.

Why did the Romans do this? It was because the Jews had dared to defy Rome. And that is the key to this whole discussion. You see, the siege of Jerusalem was ordered by Caesar specifically because the Jews had refused to accept *Caesar's* edicts, and because they refused to worship *Caesar* as God. The cause of the war had nothing to do with any grievances between Israel and her Arabic neighbors. Consequently, when tensions finally boiled over in 66 A.D. and a handful of Jewish freedom-fighters evicted the Roman garrison at Fort Antonia, Emperor Nero became enraged and commanded his troops, both homegrown and foreign, to avenge the insult to the dignity and authority of *Rome*. And that is why the destruction of Jerusalem and the Temple is properly attributed to the Romans, not to their Arabic underlings. *Had the Arabs not been a part of the Roman forces, the Romans still would have declared war on Israel, and they still would have gone forward and annihilated Jerusalem and the Temple.* And that is why the Romans are the people in view in Daniel 9:26, not the Arabs.

Unfazed by these facts, those who support the Islamic Antichrist Theory have an interesting comeback: Rome, they say, bears no blame for destroying the Temple because General Titus had specifically ordered his men not to do so. The general, it seems, wanted to

---

[11] The defeated Jewish commanders were John of Giscala and Simon Giora.

save the magnificent structure as a trophy for Rome, and when the Syrians set fire to the building, Titus actually ran to the site and tried to prevent his subordinates from damaging the House of God. But the ill-mannered Syrians had no interest in preserving Roman trophies. Instead, they were seething with greed and vengeance. So the Syrians defied their commander and broke into the Temple despite Titus' order. They then looted the Sanctuary and demolished the structure, stone by stone.

Well...it's true. Titus had indeed told his men not to harm the Temple. And the unruly Syrians had indeed rushed in and started to tear down the Sanctuary despite Titus' commands.[12] But it is *also* true that Titus — eager for pay-back and a share of the Temple treasures — soon reversed his decision and ordered his men to obliterate the Holy Place, all the way to its foundations:

> Now as soon as the army had no more people to slay, or to plunder...**Caesar** [Titus] **gave orders** that they should now demolish the entire city, and temple.[13]

The Romans then joined their Syrian comrades, finished the Temple's destruction, and killed or enslaved every Jew in sight. The city itself was obliterated. Thus, the Italians were just as guilty of destroying Jerusalem and the Sanctuary as their foreign subordinates.

Again, the Roman armies that surrounded the Jewish capital may have consisted (in large part) of Syrians and Edomites — although even that point is debated by reputable scholars[14] — but these Middle East tribesmen never would've laid siege to the city or destroyed the Temple without the resources, initiative, and leadership of the Italians. This is why Daniel, in the 7th Century B.C., referred to the future Roman marauders as the nameless "people... that **shall come**,"

---

[12] *The Wars of the Jews*, Book 6, Chap. 4, Para. 3, 6, 7.

[13] *The Wars of the Jews*, Book 7, Chap. 1, Para. 1. Also see Book 6, Chap. 6, Para. 3.

[14] For example, Professor William J. Hamblin (BYU) puts the ratio closer to 50-50. Please see: https://scholarsarchive.byu.edu/cgi/viewcontent.cgi?article=3171&context=byusq Also see the prophecy blog by Sean Osborne: https://eschatologytoday.blogspot.com/2009/02/some-thoughts-on-debunking-european.html

instead of identifying the tribes already residing in and around Judea (which Daniel easily could've done.) Local mercenaries could not have been the "people...that **shall come**," because they *already lived* in the area. Daniel obviously had another group of obscure, distant, and yet-to-come people in mind. The warriors of Italy fit this description; the Middle Eastern auxiliaries do not.

Indeed, to argue that the Arabic troops are to blame for demolishing the Temple — as opposed to their Roman masters — is like claiming that a Mafia crime boss is innocent of aggravated assault because, even though he set up the heist, provided the guns, and led the attack, most of his crew were Columbian hitmen.

Further, inasmuch as there are no records from 70 A.D. identifying the ethnic origin of each soldier who took part in the siege — in fact, there are barely 3000 source documents covering a period of 300 years and about 2 million soldiers — it's impossible to know exactly how much of that force was composed of Arabic people.[15]

What we do know is this: In 70 A.D. the legions of Rome included men from across the empire — Italy, Spain, Gaul, Germany, North Africa, Greece, etc. And all of them were under the command of an Italian Caesar and several Italian generals. It is therefore flat impossible to assign responsibility for the Temple's destruction to any one ethnic group, *except for the Italians* who indisputably instigated and led the operation.

Consequently, from a historical, legal, and practical standpoint, it was the Italians who were responsible for obliterating the "city and the sanctuary." And that means the Antichrist will hail from this *bloodline* (Hebrew *am*, v. 9:26), not from the Arabs.

---

[15] The fact that there's not enough evidence to draw absolute conclusions about the ethnicity of Roman forces in Judaea in 70 A.D. is tacitly admitted by several IAT proponents who resort to "academic consensus" to support their position. Academic consensus is a device that automatically concedes the position is weak, because if the data is truly robust and dispositive, then taking a vote on the matter is irrelevant. Instead, the one fact that is certain about who was responsible for the siege of Jerusalem is that the Italians were in charge.

IAT CLAIM #2. According to the Apocalypse, Satan will give his "throne" to the Antichrist. And since Satan's Throne was once located in (what is now) Turkey, the Antichrist must be a Turk— which means he must be a Muslim!

SUPPORT: There can be no doubt that Satan will give his throne to the Antichrist in the very near future. Speaking of the Tribulation period, Revelation 13:2 clearly states:

> Now **the beast** which I saw was like a leopard, his feet were like *the feet of* a bear, and his mouth like the mouth of a lion. **The dragon gave him** his power, **his throne,** and great authority. (NKJV)

We also know that something called "Satan's throne" was located in the city of *Pergamum* at the time that John wrote the Apocalypse:

> **Revelation 2:12-13** (NKJV) – And to the angel of the church in **Pergamos** write, "These things says He who has the sharp two-edged sword: I know your works, and where you dwell, **where Satan's throne** *is.*"

Obviously, since the city of Pergamum once was the site of "**Satan's throne**," and since Pergamum is now within the borders of **Turkey**, the Antichrist's seat of government must be located in Turkey, as well. And that means he must be a Muslim!

WHY THIS ARGUMENT IS FALSE: Despite how rational the above argument might sound, the logic collapses upon closer inspection.

In the first place, when Jesus said that Satan's throne was located in Pergamum,[16] he was not insinuating that Pergamum was literally the place where Satan held court. It was not his command post or global operations center. In fact, while several cities have served as focal points for Satan's war against God (Babylon, Nineveh, Tyre, Rome, etc.), no emperor or caliph ever ruled from Pergamum in Jesus' day

---

[16] Many believe that the "throne of Satan" cited by Jesus in Revelation 2 was a reference to Pergamum's "Altar of Zeus" (now located in Berlin, Germany), but this is unlikely because the Altar of Zeus was a temple, not a throne.

or at any other time.[17] The city never functioned as Satan's physical capital or even his "strategic headquarters" in any sense of the word.

Moreover, while several expositors have suggested that Pergamum's famous Altar of Zeus was the "throne of Satan" to which Jesus referred in Revelation 2, this is highly doubtful. In the first place, the Altar of Zeus was a building, not a throne. In the second, Jesus was concerned about the demonic doctrines that were infecting the Church (v. 14 and 15), not the enemy's furniture.

In truth, when Jesus said that "Satan's throne" was in Pergamum, he was simply using a metaphor. He was emphasizing the fact that Pergamum was filled with so much sin and depravity, the enemy's spirit dominated and "dwelled" in the city (v.13). Pergamum was a "cathedral" of demonic iniquity, a place where sin was "enthroned." That's all Jesus meant.

Consequently, the term "Satan's throne" is not a code for the enemy's seat of government or the place from which the Antichrist will rule. It is simply a figure of speech. The phrase can refer to any city or place that is drenched in debauchery. In this sense, cities like Sodom, Nineveh, Babylon, Pompeii, Tyre, Athens, and Rome — each in their heyday — also could've been described as places "where Satan's throne is." It is simply any place where sin "rules." [18]

On the other hand, when Revelation 13 says the Dragon will "give his throne" to the Beast, it means that Satan will give the Antichrist the right to rule on his behalf. It means that the devil will delegate his authority and power to his son, so that his diabolical plans can be efficiently carried out. That's the common meaning of granting a subordinate one's throne. It is more a legal reality than a physical one.[19]

---

[17] In ancient times Pergamum served as the capital of the Roman province of "Asia" (i.e., Asia Minor or present-day Turkey.) But it was never the capital of the empire. No Caesar or Caliph ever ruled from Pergamum, and thus, when combined with the above facts, it is clear that Pergamum cannot be used to anticipate the Antichrist's origin.

[18] A similar idiom is used in Jer. 1:14-15, 43:9-11, and 49:37-39 to denote a king's *authority* over a nation he rules or has conquered, not the location of his *capital city*.

[19] In fact, later in Revelation (chapter 13), when John says that Satan will "give his throne" to the Antichrist, *both* aspects of that phrasing are included: legal and physical. Satan will grant

Consequently, Revelation 2:13 does not prove the Antichrist will come from Turkey. And it certainly doesn't prove he will be a Muslim.

IAT CLAIM #3 – Several monarchs in Scripture are known by the title *king of the north*. **And all of them lived in the Middle East. Therefore, when Daniel calls the Antichrist the "king of the north," he's telling us the Antichrist will be a Middle East monarch, as well.**

SUPPORT: Daniel refers to the Antichrist as the "king of the north," at least twice in his book. One reference is explicit, the other implicit:

> **Daniel 11:21** – And in his estate [the estate of a *previous* "**king of the north**"] shall stand up a vile person [the Antichrist], to whom they shall not give the honour of the kingdom.

> **Daniel 11:40** – [A]nd the **king of the north** [the Antichrist] shall come against him like a whirlwind, with chariots, and with horsemen, and with many ships...

These verses add a lot of weight to the notion that the Antichrist will be a Middle East ruler, because every other time the Bible uses this moniker — King of the North — it denotes a sovereign who ruled in the region of Assyria, Asia Minor, Babylon, or Greece. In other words, it denotes a country within or around the Middle East.

Consequently, when Scripture calls the Antichrist the "king of the north" in Daniel 11, the Lord is telling us the Antichrist will come from a Middle East nation.

WHY THIS ARGUMENT IS FALSE: I agree that the "king of the north" in Daniel 11:21-45 is the Antichrist. However, the title, "king of the north," does not automatically mean the Antichrist comes from the Middle East, or that his country is situated on a line that runs

---

his son the *legal right* to rule on his behalf, but he will also give him the *physical empire* that Satan used to assassinate Christ, i.e., the empire of Rome.

between Jerusalem and the North Pole. Instead, it simply indicates the region of Israel through which the Antichrist's forces are likely to enter the Holy Land.[20]

This is not surprising since the tribes of Israel often designated their enemies by the choke point through which their enemies' armies had to pass. Consequently, the designation "king of the north" or "king of the south" simply identified the pathway and cities that had to be defended in the event of an invasion, *regardless* of where the opponent's homeland was actually situated.

If the designation was "north," then the first tribes to face trouble would be those in the north quadrant, Asher and Naphtali, and the topography of the ensuing battle might include the plains of Megiddo, or an elevated range like Mt. Hermon. If "south," then the tribes of Simeon and Judah were in play, and the action might start near cities like Beersheba or Hebron. In brief, the terms "king of the south" and "king of the north" were a kind of shorthand for military purposes.

Consequently, the title "king of the north" was often assigned to monarchs *whose kingdoms did not lie anywhere near* the region to the immediate north of Israel. This includes kingdoms that were positioned northwest of Israel (such as Magog - Ez. 38:15); directly east of Israel (such as Babylon - Ez.26:7); northeast of Israel (such as the Seleucid Empire - Dan. 11:6-20); or even outside the Middle East entirely (such as Greece - Dan. 11:2-4, by inference). And, yes, it also applied to kingdoms that lay directly north of Israel, such as Assyria (Zeph. 2:13).

All that was required for a monarch to be dubbed "king of the north" was for that monarch to enter the Holy Land via the northern approach (Jer. 25:26). And that's precisely how a Roman Caesar would have entered.[21] (See map below.)

---

[20] Technically speaking, magnetic compasses did not exist in the days of the Old Testament. Hence, "north" was literally "the land of darkness," while "east" was "the sunrise." The compass points mentioned above, however, are essentially accurate.

[21] In 63 B.C. Rome did, in fact, enter the Holy Land via the northern approach when Pompey's army marched to Jerusalem by way of Damascus. Later, circa 67 A.D., the V and XII Roman

Hence, the title "king of the north" in Daniel 11 does not prove the future Antichrist will be a Middle East ruler, or that his country must lie directly north of Judaea. Instead, he could simply be a Roman (an Italian) who enters Israel via the northern gateway.

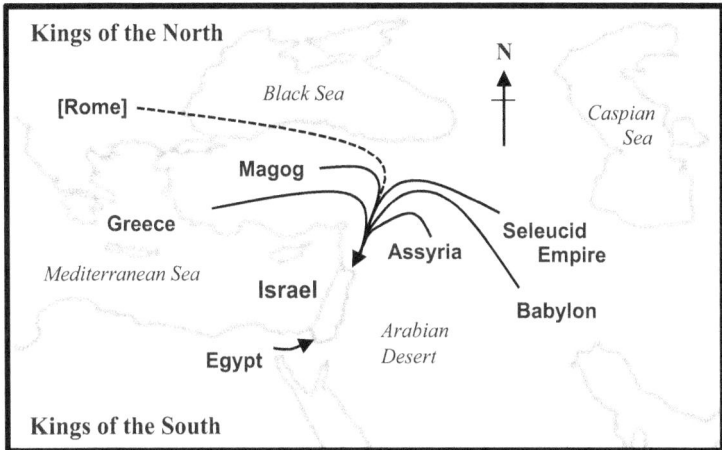

IAT CLAIM #4 – The Bible repeatedly says that the Islamic nations which surround Israel are going to be severely punished at the Battle of Armageddon. The Antichrist must therefore come from one of those nations. He must be Islamic.

SUPPORT: The Bible repeatedly says that the people of Assyria, Moab, Edom, and many other Middle East tribes, will be the greatest antagonists of the Jews in the last days (Ps. 83; Ez. 11:14-17, 35:10; Joel 3:4, etc.) It also says these people will be punished at the Battle of Armageddon for their crimes against the Jews — the very same battle where the Antichrist will be judged and sent to the Lake of Fire.

Logically, this means that the Man of Sin will emerge from one of these Arabic population centers, all of which are now Muslim. This

---

Legions also entered Israel via the northern gateway on their march to the Jewish capital and its destruction.

is especially true since the Bible places so much emphasis on their destruction by Christ, while Scripture never mentions "Rome" or "Europe" in connection with the Beast.

WHY THIS ARGUMENT IS FALSE: Unfortunately for those who subscribe to the Islamic Antichrist Theory, the above line of reasoning is grossly off-track because it contains an error in logic. That error is known as a *false equivalence*. A false equivalence occurs whenever someone claims that two things are identical, simply because they share a few characteristics.

In this case, those who support the IAT rely on just two characteristics. The first is that both the Arabs and the Antichrist will hate Israel and attempt to destroy her during the Tribulation. The second is that both the Arabs and the Antichrist will be defeated and judged at Armageddon. Can you guess what's coming? That's right! Based on this meager evidence, IAT theorists then conclude that the Antichrist will rise out of the Arabic nations, because a common hatred and a common demise (supposedly) imply a common ancestry!

This line of thinking, however, is mistaken. Nothing in Scripture explicitly connects the Antichrist to the Arabs, and such a connection is not required by any prophecy. The pertinent passages harmonize just as well if the Antichrist comes from Italy at the head of a European army, and the Arabs simply work to destroy Israel at the same moment.

Nevertheless, IAT expositors are unlikely to concede this point. Instead, they will observe that the sheer number of instances in which Arabic nations are mentioned in connection with the final battle proves the Beast will be a Muslim. The Antichrist *has to* rise from the territory of Moab, Edom, Seir, Gebal, Assyria, or Babylon, they say, because these countries are mentioned so many times in connection with end-time scriptures, while Rome and Europe are not.[22]

---

[22] According to IAT proponents, the fact that Scripture repeatedly predicts the destruction of Moab, Edom, Seir, Ammon, Dedan, Egypt, Cush, Put, Philistia, Amalek, and Lud at the return of Christ (Joel 3:11-12; Zech. 12:2, 6, 16; Ez. 25:12-16, 28:23-24; Zeph. 2, Nu. 24:17-24; Is. 25:8-11) means the Antichrist is likely to come from one of the nations in the

In response, I would first remind everyone that citing additional examples of a faulty argument cannot make that argument true, no matter how many examples are cited. *Just because CNN names a string of Eastern European gangs to prove they have overtaken organized crime, it doesn't mean that every crime boss in America is now a member of the Chechen mafia, or that no other gangs are responsible for criminal activity.*

Similarly, just because the Bible repeatedly condemns Arabic nations for their treatment of Israel and predicts their demise when Jesus returns, it doesn't *automatically* mean the Antichrist is an Arab. The fact is, the Bible never makes that assertion. It never says, "The Antichrist will come out of Egypt," or, "The Antichrist is a son of Assyria." Instead, the Bible repeatedly says the entire world will hate the Jews in the end times (Mt. 24:9), and all nations will be gathered to Armageddon (Rev. 16:14). Consequently, not only will the Arabic nations show up in Israel, but so will the forces of Russia, China, and America, *along with* the European nations of Antichrist.

Therefore, passages such as Numbers 24, Psalm 83, Isaiah 25, Zecharaiah 12, and Ezekiel 11, which are often used to support the IAT position, do not prove the Antichrist will be a Muslim. Instead, they simply chronicle some of the many participants of Armageddon, in this case, the Arabs. **They do not explicitly tie the Antichrist to the Arabic people**. And that is the critical data-point that IAT backers have missed.

Second, just because Scripture never explicitly names Europe or Rome in connection with the Antichrist's homeland, it doesn't mean he isn't from that region. The fact is, none of the prophets of Israel would've mentioned Europe or Rome in their writings because neither location was very well known to the Jews at the time those prophecies were recorded.

---

immediate vicinity of Israel (which all of these nations were.) But this assessment is pure *speculation*, because the Bible never specifically says the Antichrist will come from any of those nations. Moreover, that position flies in the face of other scriptures which clearly indicate that the Antichrist is a descendant of Rome. Please see my books, *The Antichrist* and *Empire of the Antichrist*.

For instance, in the late 700s B.C. when Isaiah recorded his visions, Europe was little more than a fragmented collection of insignificant tribes, and Rome itself was only beginning to coalesce as a kingdom under a series of semi-mythological kings. The city was virtually unknown outside of the Italian peninsula, and it was completely off the radar of the Assyrian, Babylonian, Persian, Egyptian, and Greek nation-states.

Even as late as 445 B.C., when Malachi wrote the final book of the Old Testament, Rome was still in the early phase of the republic and exerted practically no influence on Middle Eastern affairs. The prophets of Israel were essentially unaware of, and thus unconcerned with, Rome at that time.

Consequently, if the Angel (in Daniel 11) had said to the prophet, "The people of the prince that shall come will emerge from **Rome**," the name would not have registered with God's spokesman, or with his audience, the Jews. It wouldn't have made sense to either of them. So the Angel identified the Antichrist's homeland by forecasting the actions of its people: The Antichrist's people, he said, would be the ones responsible for tearing down the Temple and the city. And history tells us it was the *Romans* who did that in 70 A.D.

Therefore, to argue that the Antichrist cannot come from Rome or Europe, simply because those places are not explicitly mentioned in Scripture is, at best, an argument from silence. It carries almost no weight.

On the other hand, while the Bible never explicitly says the Antichrist's homeland is Rome, it unquestionably points to that location *geographically*. We find this marker in Daniel 8:9. In fact, Daniel's words are so clear that there's no need to guess at their meaning: the Antichrist will come from an area that lies to the **northwest** of Israel — a zone that is completely devoid of Arabic nations:

Daniel 8:9 – And out of one of them came forth a **little horn** [the Antichrist], which waxed exceeding great, toward the **south**, and toward the **east**, and toward the **pleasant land**.[23]

One look at the map below should convince any fair-minded person that the only group of nations from which a person could travel "south and east," and reach the "pleasant land" (Israel), is the European Union: France, Spain, England, Italy, et al. — not Egypt, Libya, Saudi Arabia, Jordan, Iraq, or any other Arabic nation.

Dan. 8:9 – The Antichrist must travel "south and east" to reach Israel

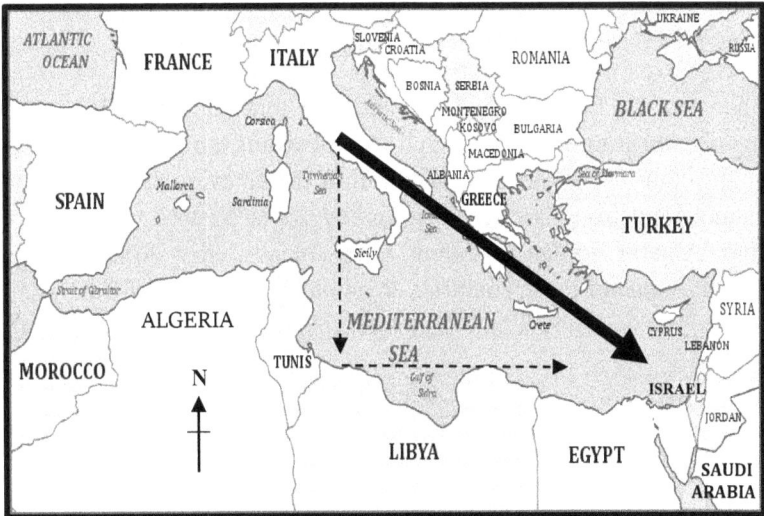

In my opinion, this map is non-negotiable. It is non-negotiable because it portrays exactly what Scripture describes. The Antichrist will come out of Europe because that is the only location that would require a "south and east" journey to get to Judaea. And that same point of origin

---

[23] In Scripture (generally speaking) Israel is the axis-point for compass directions. However, there are certain cases where Israel is not the origin or hub for a set of directions. (See, for example, Gen. 4:16; Ex. 10:19; Dan. 8:4; etc.) In the above instance, the text clearly indicates that Israel is the *terminus* for the Antichrist, not his origin (verses 9-12). Therefore, the origination-point for the direction, "south and east," must be located somewhere outside of Israel, that is, somewhere to the "north and west" of the "pleasant land."

is confirmed by such things as the *identity of the people* who destroyed the Temple in 70 A.D., the *Genesis 3:15 Pattern*, the principle of *divine retribution*, the concept known as *Three to the Cross*,[24] and many other lines of evidence. (Please see my books, *Empire of the Antichrist* and *The Antichrist,* for a complete discussion of these concepts.)

In addition, Europe is quickly descending into a new and frightening phase of anti-Semitism. Nationalist factions are persecuting the Jews as never before (at least, not since Nazi Germany), Jewish families are being forced to flee the Continent in droves, and European governments — including those of Switzerland, France, Spain, Germany, and Greece — are consistently taking sides against the Jews in the midst of international disputes.[25] In other words, the spirit of Antichrist is bursting across Europe.

Therefore, in light of Daniel's statement that the Little Horn must travel "**south and east**" to reach the "**pleasant land**," the Antichrist could come from the European Continent or even Britain. But he cannot come from Saudi Arabia, Turkey, Syria, Yemen, Qatar, Egypt, Iraq, Algeria, Jordan, Lebanon, Gaza, or any other Arabic nation, because none of those countries are situated northwest of Canaan.[26]

---

[24] *Three to the Cross* refers to the fact that, according to Daniel 9:24-26, the final empire had to be in existence not later than the year the Messiah was crucified and "cut off." This is because all **three** empires in Daniel's "visions and prophecy" (chapters 8 and 9) had to appear within Daniel's first 69 weeks, which began in 445 B.C. and ended at the **Cross** in 32 A.D. Please see my book, *Empire of the Antichrist,* for a full discussion of this concept.

[25] For example, see: www.jta.org/2018/06/13/united-states/un-general-assembly-condemns-israel-gaza-violence

[26] To be fair, one could argue that Turkey (or at least part of it) lies northwest of Israel. However, Turkey is so wide that half the country also lies *northeast* of the Jewish state. Therefore, the most accurate way to describe Turkey's position is to say that it lies **north** of Canaan. And if that's true, then it follows that Turkey cannot be the homeland of the Antichrist, because the "little horn" travels **south and east** to reach the Jews, not merely south.

IAT CLAIM #5. The book of Revelation clearly implies that the Antichrist has the DNA of the Babylonian, Medo-Persian, and Greek peoples. He must therefore be a son of the Middle East.

SUPPORT: Revelation 13 seems to indicate that the Beast is a "composite" of the Babylonian, Medo-Persian, and Greek people. His body consists of the same three beasts that Daniel used to represent the above three empires — the lion, the bear, and the leopard:

> **Revelation 13:1-2** – And I stood upon the sand of the sea, and saw a **beast** [the Antichrist] rise up out of the sea... And the beast which I saw was like unto a **leopard**, and his feet were as the feet of a **bear**, and his mouth as the mouth of a **lion**: and the dragon gave him his power, and his seat, and great authority.

Consequently, the Antichrist must be a descendant of the people who lived in those areas. And that means he must be a Muslim, because Islam now dominates those very same territories.

WHY THIS ARGUMENT IS FALSE: The various components of the Beast's body in Revelation 13:2 do not reflect the Antichrist's geneaology, religion, ethnic group, territorial base, or nationality. Instead, they reflect his **aggressive, violent nature**. They tell us he will be the commander-in-chief of a ten-nation military alliance that will exhibit unmatched **speed, power, and cunning**.

How do we know this is the proper way to assess the symology of the lion, the bear, and the leopard here in the Apocalypse? Because that is what the same symology conveyed when it first appeared in the book of Daniel (Rules 1 and 4).

As you may recall, the image of a winged lion in Daniel 7:4 symbolized the fact that King Nebuchadnezzar soared over his enemies, and that all military power was vested in him alone (v. 2:37-38; 4:22). It meant that Nebuchadnezzar was incredibly bold in war and extremely proud in peace. The winged lion did not mean that Nebuchadnezzar was ethnically Middle Eastern.[27]

Similarly, the image of a lopsided bear in Daniel 7:5 meant that the armies of Medo-Persia would be composed of two "unequal" columns (one stronger than the other), yet they would be so massive and powerful (like an enormous bear), they would devour all their opponents (v. 7:5).

Again, in Daniel 7:6, the image of a leopard with four wings and four heads meant that Alexander the Great would strike his enemies with blinding speed (four wings), unbeatable tactics (four heads), and incredible strength (the essence of a leopard). It did not mean that Alexander was necessarily Greek or Macedonian.

Consequently, the image of a Beast in Revelation 13 with the mouth of a lion, the feet of a bear, and the body of a leopard, do not symbolize the Antichrist's nationality, religion, or ethnicity. Instead, they symbolize his speed, power, and brilliance in battle. **He will be more quick, vicious, and sly than Babylon, Medo-Persia, and Greece *put together*.**

If this was not true — if the components of the Beast had anything to do with the Antichrist's religion, ethnicity, or national origin — we'd be forced to conclude the Antichrist will be either a "Greek–Turk–Persian–Arab" by ethnicity, or a "Greek Orthodox–Muslim" by religion, both of which are meaningless constructs.

Therefore, nothing in Revelation 13:2 speaks to the Antichrist's race, citizenship, or religious affiliation (except, perhaps, to acknowledge

---

[27] Daniel uses the image of a lion as a motif for Nebuchadnezzar. But he does this to indicate the king's *ferocity*, not to indicate that he's ethnically Babylonian. For example, Jesus—who is clearly not a Babylonian—is also represented as a lion in Bible prophecy to indicate the Lord's *ferocity*, not his ethnicity (he is the *Lion of Judah* in Gen. 49:8-10 and Rev. 5:5). Even Satan—who is also not a Babylonian—is compared to a lion to indicate his *ferocity* (1 Pet. 5:8). Likewise, several modern states claim the lion as their national symbol (e.g., Britain, Belgium, Iran, Finland, etc.) because the lion signifies *ferocity*, not ethnicity. Consequently, the 'mouth of a lion' in Rev. 13:2 does not signal the Beast's religion, ethnicity, or nationality. It simply means he is absolutely ferocious and deadly. The Beast is a warmonger, not a Babylonian.

his association with Gentile empires, as opposed to Israel.) Instead, this imagery tells us the Antichrist will be endowed with total authority over his forces, those forces will be massive and powerful, and the Antichrist will use them to overwhelm his opponents with unequalled speed, strength, and tactical brilliance.[28]

IAT CLAIM #6. According to Daniel, the Antichrist's kingdom will be defined by the borders that once defined the kingdom of Antiochus IV. Therefore, since that territory is now inhabited almost entirely by Muslims, the Antichrist must be a Muslim.

<u>SUPPORT</u>: The prophet Daniel once predicted that a "king of fierce countenance" would someday rise in the Middle East and wreak havoc in Israel:

> **Daniel 8:23-24** – And in the latter time of their kingdom, when the transgressors are come to the full, a **king of fierce countenance**, and understanding dark sentences, shall stand up. And his power shall be mighty, but not by his own power: and he shall destroy wonderfully, and shall prosper, and practise, and shall destroy the mighty and the holy people.

Many expositors identify this king — whom Daniel also calls the "little horn" (v. 9) — as Antiochus Epiphanes. This is because Antiochus' reign of terror in Judaea from 168–164 B.C. seemed to fulfill much of Daniel's prophecy. Antiochus was a thoroughly brutal

---

[28] Some IAT theorists believe the components of the Beast's body (lion-bear-leopard) signal the nations that will join his military alliance, as opposed to signaling the military qualities of the man and his forces (i.e., speed, power, and ferocity in battle.) However, if that was true, then the final empire would consist of the most unlikely bedfellows: Greece and Turkey (who are still bitter enemies), and Iraq and Iran (who are also fierce rivals). Further, if the composite features of an empire indicate it has absorbed all the previous empires—as several IAT theorists contend—then to be consistent, the second beast in Daniel (Medo-Persia) should be a bear with *some lion features* (because Medo-Persia conquered and absorbed Babylon), and the third beast (Greece) should be a leopard with *some features of a bear and a lion* (because the Greeks conquered and absorbed Babylon and Medo-Persia.) But, of course, that's not what Scripture says. Instead, each animal is separate and distinct, and only the fourth is said to include the attributes of the others—their speed, power, and ferocity.

tyrant who took control of Judaea, outlawed Judaism, tortured the Jews, and desecrated the Temple. He showed no mercy to anyone. In fact, he was such a megalomaniac that he subjugated not only Judaea but also much of the territory that would later comprise the first Islamic Caliphate.

Consequently, since the Antichrist is widely believed to be the final fulfillment of the Daniel 8 prophecy, he must emerge from the same territory that was once controlled by Antiochus. And almost everyone in that region today is a Muslim.

WHY THIS ARGUMENT IS FALSE: The notion that Daniel's "king of fierce countenance" is Antiochus IV is patently false. Therefore, the borders that once defined Antiochus' kingdom cannot be used to deduce the territory from which the future Antichrist will emerge.

How do we know that Daniel's "king of fierce countenance" is not Antiochus IV? Because the Angel who interprets the vision specifically says the "king of fierce countenance" is a monarch who will appear in the "latter time":

> **Daniel 8:23** — And in the **latter time** of their kingdom, when the transgressors are come to the full, a **king of fierce countenance**…shall stand up.

In other words, the "king of fierce countenance" in this passage is someone who will come to power during the *Tribulation*. He will come during the "**latter time**," a technical phrase that always denotes all (or part) of the 70th Week of Daniel. He will come when mankind has become so depraved and sinful that our planet is finally ready for the judgments of the Apocalypse, i.e., when the "transgressions" of mankind have "come to the full."

Neither of those conditions were satisfied at the time of Antiochus, nor have they been satisfied at any time since. Therefore, from verse 23 forward, the passage can only be speaking about the future Antichrist, not some historical monster like Antiochus. And that means the areas that were controlled by Antiochus are useless for predicting the Antichrist's origin, because Antiochus is not in the picture.[29]

The parallel statement in verse 19, which discusses the timing of the "king of fierce countenance" and his rise to power, reinforces this:

> **Daniel 8:19** — And he [the Angel] said, Behold, I will make thee know **what shall be in the last end** of the indignation: for at the time appointed the end shall be.

It doesn't get much clearer than that. The final part of Daniel's vision is an account of things that "shall be in the last end." It is a forecast of **end-time events**. It will be when God's "indignation" has reached its limit, and "the transgressors are come to the full." It will be at the end of the age, during the Tribulation. Then, and only then, will the "king of fierce countenance" arise:

> **Daniel 8:23** — And in the **latter time** of their kingdom...
> a **king of fierce countenance**...shall stand up.

The "king of fierce countenance" must therefore be the future Antichrist, not the historical Antiochus. And that means neither Antiochus, nor the borders of his empire, can be used to predict where the Beast will come from.

Please note: Like many other Antichrist archetypes, such as Nebuchadnezzar and Alexander, I agree that several of Antiochus's traits parallel those of the Beast. For example, in apparent fulfillment of some of the Antichrist prophecies, Antiochus desecrated the Temple, outlawed Judaism, and persecuted any Jew who resisted his authority.

---

[29] In an attempt to strengthen the notion that Antiochus IV is the "king of fierce countenance" in verse 8:23, several expositors claim that Daniel 11:21-35 *also* describes the reign of Antiochus, and that these chapters therefore support the "Antiochus" theory in tandem. However, that position cannot be true for one simple reason: The last emergence of a "king of the north" occurs in v. 21, meaning that v. 21 is where the narrative breaks from the ancient kings to the final Antichrist. And since the king in the preceding verse (v. 20) is a monarch who died *before* Antiochus came to power (undoubtedly, Seleucus Philopater), then no part of Daniel 11 can be speaking about Antiochus. Note carefully: The king in v. 21 is said to be a commoner (Old English, "vile person," that is, a person of low birth), and thus cannot be a member of royalty (he will not be given "the honour of the kingdom.") This immediately rules out Antiochus, who was a Macedonian prince and came from a long line of Seleucid kings. (The CEV Bible conveys this concept quite well in modern English.)

Yet Antiochus also failed to match a number of key Antichrist details. For example, Antiochus did not invade Judaea from the northwest (Dan. 8:9), nor did he "understand dark sentences," which is to say, speak in parables (Dan. 8:23; cf Ps. 78:2), nor did he claim to be higher than the Prince of the host, which is to say, higher than Jesus (Dan. 8:25), nor does any sequence of events in the Second Century B.C. fit the 2300 days mentioned in verse 8:14. And, again, Antiochus is certainly not a "latter time" figure, as required by verse 8:23. Therefore, Antiochus cannot be the "little horn" of Daniel 8.

Jesus himself recognized this reality and accounted for it during the Olivet discourse (his lengthy sermon on the end times) when he told the disciples that the "little horn's" entrance into the Holy of Holies — in fulfillment of Daniel 8:11 — still lay in the *future:*

> **Daniel 8:11** — Yea, he magnified himself even to the prince of the host, and by him the daily sacrifice was taken away, and the place of the sanctuary was cast down.

> **Matthew 24:15-16** — When ye therefore shall see the abomination of desolation, spoken of by Daniel the prophet, stand in the holy place, (whoso readeth, let him understand:) Then let them which be in Judaea flee into the mountains.

Clearly, from Jesus' perspective, the Abomination of Desolation had not yet occurred. Therefore, since Jesus made this statement in about 32 A.D., any monarch who reigned prior to that year, such as Antiochus (215–164 B.C.), could not have been the "king of fierce countenance" mentioned by Daniel.

Nevertheless, despite this clear teaching, many IAT proponents refuse to accept it. Instead, they will often respond with another mistaken idea: They will observe that the "little horn" of verse 8 emerges from one of the four Greek kingdoms that immediately succeeded Alexander the Great—which would effectively place the Little Horn (a.k.a., the "king of fierce countenance") in the era of the Seleucid kings, about 150 years before Christ!

> **Daniel 8:8-9** — Therefore the he goat waxed very great: and when he was strong, the great horn [Alexander] was broken; and for it came up **four notable ones** [four Greek kings] toward the four winds of heaven. And out of **one of them** came forth a **little horn** [supposedly Antiochus]…

In the minds of most IAT supporters, this statement proves that Antiochus is in view, because one of the "four notable" kings who succeeded Alexander was a man by the name of Seleucus (358-281 B.C.), and Antiochus came from the Seleucid line.

Unfortunately for IAT advocates, this analysis is also incorrect because verses 8 and 9 do not say the Antichrist will emerge from one of the "four notable ones," they say he will emerge from one of the "four winds of heaven":

> **Daniel 8:8-9** — Therefore the he goat waxed very great: and when he was strong, the great horn was broken; and for it came up four notable ones toward the **four winds of heaven**. And out of **one of them** came forth a **little horn**, which waxed exceeding great, toward the south, and toward the east, and toward the pleasant land.

This might take a moment to process, especially for people whose primary language is English. But for those who are fluent in Hebrew, the *natural* reading is that the Little Horn comes from one of the "four winds of heaven," not from one of the "four notable ones." This is because Hebrew grammar connects the noun being modified (in this case, "one of them") to its closest antecedent (one of the "four winds of heaven.")[30] Thus, in the original language, the meaning of Daniel 8:8-9 is that the "little horn" will emerge from a dark and distant land which was unknown to Daniel at that moment, metaphorically, one of the "four winds of heaven."

Indeed, it is *because* this passage pertains to the Antichrist's geographic origin — as opposed to his ethnic origin — that Scripture

---

[30] In Hebrew, the "**closest antecedent**" rule, plus the specific **gender** and **number** of the relevant Hebrew words, prove this is the proper interpretation of verses 8 and 9. For a good analysis see: https://revelationbyjesuschrist.com/out-of-one-of-them/

immediately clears up the ambiguity of the phrase "one of the four winds of heaven" by revealing the exact direction from which the Little Horn will emerge: verse 9 says he will come from a place to the *northwest* of Israel (he must travel "south" and "east" to reach the "pleasant land.") In contrast to this description, Antiochus' capital, a city called *Antioch*, was located directly *north* of Israel, not northwest.

Consequently, the actual information provided by Daniel 8 is that: 1) the Antichrist will rise *after* the time of the "four notable ones," 2) he will come from a place that was unknown to Daniel at that moment (from one of the "four winds of heaven," specifically, from a place to the *northwest* of Canaan), and 3) he will come in the "latter time," that is, during the future Tribulation. Anything else is speculation, and prone to error.

IAT CLAIM #7. The Antichrist will belong to a religion that denies the deity of Christ, such as the religion of Islam.

SUPPORT: The resemblance between the "anti-christ" religion described by John in one of his letters and the religion of Islam is uncanny. In fact, it seems to suggest that Islam and the religion described by John are one-and-the-same.

For example, in 1 John 2:22, the apostle says that the "anti-christ" religion will "deny that Jesus is the Christ" (i.e., deny that Jesus is the one-and-only Christ), and/or "deny the Father and the Son" (i.e., deny that Jesus is the only begotten Son of God, and is therefore equally as divine as the Father.) Such a religion, according to John, is indisputably "anti-christ."

Consequently, the Man of Sin could be a Muslim because the religion of Islam specifically denies that Jesus is God's Son. And it denies that Jesus is divine. Jesus might be a "good man" and a "prophet," but he is not God Almighty, according to Muslims.

WHY THIS ARGUMENT IS FALSE: If 1 John 2:22 was the only criterion by which to evaluate the Antichrist, then, yes, the Beast of

Revelation could be a Muslim. There's no question that Islam denies that Jesus is God's Son.

But then again, under the same criterion, the Antichrist could also be a Jew, a Sikh, a Mormon, a Deist, an Atheist, or even a Buddhist, because *all* of these religions deny the supreme divinity of Jesus, as well. All of them deny that Jesus was, and is, an equal member of the triune Godhead. Therefore, this argument does little for the IAT theory, except to show that the theory does not contradict 1 John 2:22. That's hardly a fact upon which to build a solid hypothesis.

Instead, based upon the well-supported *Roman Antichrist* position, and John's definition of what constitutes the antichrist spirit, a more likely scenario is that the Beast is a Roman Catholic who embraces the "anti-Christ" catechisms of Rome, which insist that other men, besides Jesus, either possess the divine nature or can eventually attain it. After all, the Vatican routinely declares that certain human beings are both "holy" and "divine," and are therefore deserving of mankind's prayers and worship. (And if worshipping a man isn't "anti-Christ," then I don't know what is.)

These Catholic "super-humans" include the popes, the apostles, an ever-growing roster of Catholic saints, and Mary, the mother of Jesus.[31] Indeed, it wouldn't take much (especially in the current spiritual climate) for a "Catholic" Antichrist to arrogate this concept and declare that he, too, is divine, a statement he would then follow by taking a trip to Jerusalem, where he would enter the new Jewish Temple, sit on a throne, and announce that he — not Jesus — is the true God of the universe:

> **2 Thessalonians 2:3-4** — Let no man deceive you by any means: for that day shall not come, except there come a falling away first, and that man of sin be revealed, the son of perdition; Who opposeth and exalteth himself above all that is called God, or that is worshipped; so that **he as God**

---

[31] See *Catechism of the Catholic Church, 2ⁿᵈ Edition* (2000), paragraphs 828, 957, 962, 966-969, 971, 986, etc.

sitteth in the temple of God, shewing himself that he is God.

> **Daniel 11:31, 36** — And arms shall stand on his part, and they shall pollute the sanctuary of strength [the Temple], and shall take away the daily sacrifice, and **they shall place the abomination that maketh desolate** [the image of the Beast]... And the king shall do according to his will; **and he shall exalt himself, and magnify himself above every god**, and shall speak marvellous things against the God of gods...

In my opinion, a Roman Antichrist could easily fulfill these prophecies. But no "Muslim Antichrist" would even think of committing such blasphemous acts, because each of those acts would constitute a blatant violation of one of Islam's most sacred doctrines, the *Shahada*, which states: "There is no god but Allah."

On the other hand, a Roman Antichrist would have no problem claiming to be divine because Roman kingpins have been doing this for centuries. The list includes such heavies as Tiberius, Caligula, Nero, Domitian, Decius, Pope Boniface, Pope Leo VIII, Pope John Paul II, and Pope Pius V. All these denizens of Rome claimed to be on equal terms with the Almighty, or to hold his unique prerogatives. All of them claimed to either rule for God, speak for God, or actually be God.[32]

Therefore, based on the specifics of Daniel 11 and 2 Thessalonians 2, the Antichrist could be a Roman, but he could not be a Muslim.

IAT CLAIM #8. The Antichrist will come out of Saudi Arabia, because Saudi Arabia is actually the "Whore of Babylon," and the Beast "carries" this Whore.

SUPPORT: Saudi Arabia is the center of Islam, and the country appears to match several characteristics of the Whore of Babylon

---

[32] See, for example: https://amazingdiscoveries.org/R-Pope_Rome_blasphemy_power_Jesus

mentioned in Revelation 17: the nation is phenomenally wealthy (v. 4), its religious leaders hate Christians and Jews (v. 6), and the country is home to Mecca, a "great city" that serves as the focal point of a global, anti-Christian religion (v. 18).

Obviously, when taken together, these details prove that Saudi Arabia is the Whore of Babylon. And that means the Antichrist has to be a Muslim, because according to verse 17:3 the Whore of Babylon and the Beast are intimately connected — one sits upon the other!

WHY THIS ARGUMENT IS FALSE: Unfortunately, this interpretation (like several other IAT interpretations) requires its adherents to either ignore or misconstrue the explicit teachings of Scripture.

To review, the Bible specifically says the Whore of Babylon:

- Is a city — not a nation (vv. 16:19, 17:18, 18:10)

- Sits on seven hills[33] (v. 17:9)

- Ruled the kings of the earth in John's day (v. 17:18)

- Served as the execution site of at least two apostles (v. 18:20)

- Exhibited global power in three key areas: commerce, government, and religion (v. 16:19, and chapters 17 and 18)

In contrast to these explicit teachings:

- Saudi Arabia is a nation, not a city.

- Neither Saudi Arabia nor its religious capital, Mecca, sits on seven hills. (Traditionally, Mecca was associated with only five nearby hills — not seven — and the city never "sat" on

---

[33] There can be no question that "hills" are intended, as opposed to "mountains," because a city can sit on seven hills; it cannot sit on seven mountains. The relevant Greek word, *ore*, can mean either hill or mountain, depending on context (*cf.* Mt. 5:14 and Lk. 4:29).

any of them. Instead, it lay in a valley contained by them.)[34]

- Neither Saudi Arabia nor Mecca ruled the kings of the earth in John's day, or at any other time.

- No apostle was ever executed in Mecca, or anywhere else in the Saudi peninsula.[35]

- And, although Saudi Arabia and Mecca currently exert some influence over global commerce and the religion of Islam, they do not — and never have — exercised the power of global government.

Consequently, Revelation 17 fails to connect the Antichrist to Islam, Saudi Arabia, or Mecca.

IAT CLAIM #9. According to Daniel, the empire which produces the Antichrist will exhibit three distinct characteristics:

- **It will arrive after the empire of Greece.**

- **It will "stomp" its enemies out of existence.**

- **It will conquer the territories of Nebuchadnezzar, Darius, and Alexander.**

All of these characteristics are true of the Islamic Caliphate; they are not all true of Rome.

---

[34] The five traditional hills of Mecca are Ajyad, Abu Qubays, Quayqan, Hira, and Thawr. A good internet search will show that ancient Mecca lay in the valley behind these peaks, it did not "sit" on them. See, for example, https://www.britannica.com/place/Mecca Also see: https://www.architecturelab.net/a-building-boom-in-mecca-sacred-center-has-created-a-dazzling-high-tech-21st-century-pilgrimage/

[35] No historical records, artifacts, or Church traditions place any of the twelve apostles (or the apostle Paul) in the Arabian Peninsula at the time of their death.

SUPPORT: The first characteristic that defines the Antichrist's empire is that it will come after the empire of Greece. This is clearly stated in Daniel 7:

> **Daniel 7:7** — After this [the "leopard" of Greece] I saw in the night visions, and behold a **fourth beast**, dreadful and terrible, and strong exceedingly; and it had great iron teeth.

Clearly, the Islamic empire — having started in 632 A.D., about eight hundred years after the Greek Empire began to unravel — fulfills this requirement.

Second, the empire that will produce the Antichrist is predicted to conquer all of its enemies, and then annihilate their populations, if they refuse to be subjugated:

> **Daniel 2:40** — And the fourth kingdom shall be strong as iron… [and it shall] break in pieces and bruise.

> **Daniel 7:7** — [A]nd behold a fourth beast, dreadful and terrible… it devoured and brake in pieces, and stamped the residue with the feet of it.

These characteristics indisputably point to the Islamic Caliphate (actually a series of caliphates that were empowered between 632–1258 A.D.) Whenever the caliphate defeated a foe on the battlefield, it then wiped out all traces of the enemy's social, religious, and political order, and replaced those with Shariah law and Islam. Nothing was left of the enemy's former identity.

On the other hand, the Romans never took their conquests to such extremes. Instead, they generally left the civil and religious infrastructure of their opponents intact.

Last but not least, Daniel 2:40 again points to the Islamic Caliphate by stating that the Fourth Kingdom will conquer and absorb the territories of "all the other" kingdoms. In other words, it will commandeer and incorporate the territories once ruled by Babylon, Medo-Persia, and Greece.

This is something the Islamic Caliphate did, as it rapidly spread its dominion throughout what is now Turkey, Iran, Iraq, and Saudi Arabia. Yet, aside from western Turkey, the Romans never subjugated or incorporated any of those territories.

In view of all these facts, Daniel's Fourth Kingdom must have been the Islamic Caliphate *phase one*, and the Antichrist, as ruler of *phase two*, must be Islamic, as well.

WHY THIS ARGUMENT IS FALSE: Unfortunately for those who support the Islamic Antichrist Theory, this argument is dead wrong on all three counts:

1. In the first place, **Rome** was the empire that succeeded Greece, not the Islamic Caliphate. This one fact, by itself, is devastating to the IAT because *each empire is supposed to replace its immediate predecessor*. It is not supposed to arrive almost a thousand years after the preceding empire has ceased to exist, as is proffered by those who claim the Islamic Caliphate "succeeded" the Greek Empire. Indeed, the unbroken transition from one empire to the next is signaled by the fact that *no vertical break exists* between the components of Nebuchadnezzar's statue. Each of the four parts — head, chest, torso, legs — flows seamlessly into the next, indicating an unbroken sequence on the timeline of history.[36]

2. Next, the idea that Islam was the only empire to break other nations in pieces and "stamp the residue" is wrong. The Romans did this too.

---

[36] IAT proponents are quick to point out that the smooth flow of the statue from one part to the next doesn't necessarily indicate an uninterrupted flow on the timeline of history: The legs of iron (Rome, phase 1) flow into the feet of iron and clay (Rome, phase 2), yet there's a gap of 1500 years in real-time between the two!

Well, that's true. However, the legs and feet belong to the *same empire*. They represent the same entity. And that means *there should not be a gap between the legs and feet, regardless of how much time passes between them*. Otherwise, the empire count would be thrown into confusion. It would change from the stated "four" (v. 2:40) to "four + one," or "three + two," or "five," etc.

Further, the principle known as *Three to the Cross* proves that the final empire had to appear after Greece, but before the Crucifixion in A.D. 32., and Rome is the only empire that meets this criteria. (Please see note 22.)

Let's take a look at this. The phrases "[to] break in pieces and bruise," and "[to] stamp the residue," generally mean to annihilate the *military forces* of one's enemies and offer no quarter. Yet even if we expand that phrase to include the eradication of an entire culture, religion, or society, then Rome still seems to be in view, not the Islamic Caliphate. Why? Because it was the Romans who, in 70 A.D., completely "bruised," "stamped," and "broke" the most pivotal nation in prophecy: Israel.

As students of prophecy know, it was the Romans — not the Muslims — who annihilated the city of Jerusalem, levelled the Temple, and killed over one million Jews. It was the Romans who then evicted every remaining survivor from Judaea and caused the tragic 1900-year dispersal of the Jews among the nations. Worst of all, it was the Romans who savagely beat and crucified the Son of God, a man whom they themselves had declared to be innocent (Luke 23:13-16). In other words, the Romans are the ones who "bruised" the Savior, "broke in pieces" the most pivotal city in prophecy, and then "stamped the residue" of Israel with its feet, just as Daniel predicted.

The Islamic Caliphate, on the other hand, never destroyed the Jewish nation, or the Holy Temple, or the Son of God — nor could it have done so — *because it arrived almost six hundred years after Judaea had ceased to exist!*

Furthermore, while the Romans generally did not take their conquests to the extremes alluded to in Daniel 7:7 (they usually allowed their enemies to retain their religious, political, and social infrastructures, so the population could be efficiently taxed) they had no qualms about wiping an entire people-group off the face of the earth if the situation required.

In 146 B.C., for example, the Romans utterly wiped out the city of Carthage and took control of the Carthaginian Empire.

A short time later, in 71 B.C., the Romans decimated the forces of Spartacus (during the great slave rebellion), and then crucified some 6,000 survivors along the Appian Way. Nothing was left of the Resistance.

Indeed, genocide seems to have been the go-to option whenever Rome faced a troublesome population. Take, for example, the Suebi tribe in 58 B.C. (35,000 killed), or the Tencteri and Usipetes tribes in 55 B.C. (150,000 killed), or Ilurgia, Spain (eradicated), or Numantia, Spain (eradicated), or the Eburones tribe in 53 B.C. (eradicated), etc.

Thus, the empire described in Daniel 7, is almost certainly Rome, not the Islamic Caliphate, especially when the destruction of God's beloved Son, people, and city — the three most critical entities in all of prophecy — is taken into account.

3. Third, and perhaps most devastating of all to the Islamic Antichrist Theory, any attempt to prove that Islam was the Fourth Empire of Daniel because it conquered the territories of Babylon, Medo-Persia, and Greece is a canard. It is a bogus argument because the Bible never attributes that act to the fourth empire of Daniel, or to any other empire.

I know that might sound like an audacious claim, especially to those who support the IAT. But the New King James Version of Daniel 2:40, which is used by IAT theorists to make their case, *is not an accurate translation of the text.* Specifically, the original Hebrew of Daniel 2:40 does not say the Fourth Kingdom will "crush and shatter **all the others** [i.e., all the other empires]," as IAT theorists would have us believe. Instead, it simply says the Fourth Kingdom will "crush and shatter." [37]

This is significant. Indeed, it is actually *devastating* to the Islamic Antichrist Theory, because the last three words in that sentence — "**all the others**" — were added by the NKJV editors. They do not appear in the original manuscripts. And that means the IAT relies

---

[37] Bible versions such as the KJV, YLT, and KJ3, stay true to the original text of Daniel 2:40. For example, the KJV properly translates the verse as: "[S]hall it [the final empire] break in pieces and bruise." Period.

(in part) on words that don't even exist!

Again, the actual text of Daniel 2:40 does not say the Fourth Empire will conquer the previous three. It simply says the Fourth Empire will "crush and shatter." Properly understood, this simply means the Fourth Empire will defeat or repel all of its enemies, and it will never be shattered itself. Just like iron — a metal which is able to break or repel all other substances and all other metals — Daniel's Fourth Empire will break or repel all of its foes, regardless of what any foe is "made of." That's all the original text means. It does not say (or even imply) that the Fourth Empire will conquer and absorb the territories of Babylon, Medo-Persia, and Greece:

> **Daniel 2:40** (KJ3) – And the fourth kingdom shall be as strong as iron. Inasmuch as iron crushes and smashes all things [i.e., all other substances], and as the iron that shatters all these [i.e., shatters every other kind of metal], it will crush and shatter. [38]

This is a perfect description of Rome, the empire that was never shattered, subjugated, or replaced by any rival, regardless of what any rival was made of.

Consequently, the fact that Islam commandeered the territories of Greece, Medo-Persia, and Babylon is immaterial. It has absolutely no bearing on the identity of the Fourth Empire. Instead, the text of Daniel 2:40 actually points to the kingdom of Caesar. As the empire of unbreakable iron, Rome's collapse was *not* caused by a more powerful army, but by decay from within. The Romans were so powerful, in fact, that no enemy ever broke up their empire, enslaved them, or displaced them as rulers of the Mediterranean world. Instead, every would-be conqueror was either flat destroyed or held in check, just as the prophecy specifies.[39]

---

[38] The parallel construction of the first and second clauses — **"as iron crushes...all things"** and **"as the iron that shatters all these,"** — requires the comma in the second clause to be placed after the words **"all these,"** not before. Observing this basic rule of grammar prevents the verbiage from saying something it actually doesn't.

[39] Here, I'm speaking about the Roman Empire from 27 B.C. to 395 A.D., and the Western Roman Empire (i.e., the half that retained its Roman heritage) from 395 to 476 A.D.

The Islamic Caliphate, on the other hand — and in contradiction to the above prophetic specifications — *did not* prove unbreakable against all its enemies, but shattered *instantly* in 1258 A.D. after suffering a stunning defeat at the hands of the Mongols at the notorious Battle of Baghdad.

Likewise, the Ottoman Empire (another candidate for the Islamic kingdom that will supposedly be revived in the end times and produce the Antichrist) did not prove unbreakable against all of its enemies, but was catastrophically destroyed by the Allied Powers in World War I.[40]

Therefore, the idea that Islam is the Fourth Kingdom because the caliphate conquered the geographic regions of Babylon, Medo-Persia, and Greece is bogus. That act is never stated as an element of the prophecy. It therefore cannot be used to make the case for an Islamic Antichrist.

[Note: Although some IAT proponents cite the victory of Parthia over Crassus in 53 B.C. to prove that Rome was not invincible, the full story actually negates that allegation. First, Rome was not an empire at that time. Second, Parthia did not win any territory from the Romans in this battle. Third, the rule of Rome did not collapse as a result of the battle. And fourth, the Parthians were sufficiently convinced of Roman power (by 20 B.C.) to sign a non-aggression pact with Emperor Augustus. The treaty was considered (by many) to be a great political triumph, and for the next eighty years the Parthians stayed out of the Roman provinces. Thus, in accordance with Daniel 2, Parthia never broke or conquered the Roman Empire, nor did they supplant the Italians as rulers of the ancient world. Instead, Rome remained "un-shattered" by its enemies and continued to "stomp" its opponents into submission.

Similarly, while it's true that the Battle of Ravenna (476 A.D.) brought the Roman Empire to an end, this event was not the cause of Rome's demise — it was the validation of it. For at least a century, Rome had been disintegrating like a rusty piece of iron, thanks to its own moral decay, political corruption, administrative incompetence, and military decline. Hence, Odoacer's victory over Romulus in 476 — a two-day mugging that was over before it started — merely notarized Rome's death certificate. Significantly, in the wake of this battle neither Odoacer's tribe, the Heruli, nor any other faction ever replaced the Romans as the new and uncontested rulers of what had been the empire's territory (i.e., Europe, the Mediterranean coastlands, and the Near East.)]

[40] According to historian Elie Kedourie: "At the Armistice of Mudros, signed on 30 October 1918, the Sick Man of Europe [the Ottoman Empire]…finally died. For all his alleged sickness, however, the Sick Man did not die of disease but was **violently destroyed** in a long and bitter war…" [Boldface added.] See https://www.jstor.org/stable/259848?seq=1 "The End of the Ottoman Empire," *Journal of Contemporary History*, vol. 3, no. 4, 1968, pp. 19-28.

IAT CLAIM #10. The fact that all four sections of Nebuchadnezzar's statue collapse *at the same time* means that the Babylonian, Medo-Persian, and Greek empires (the first three sections) *must be a part of the Antichrist's empire (the fourth section).* And since the people who live in those territories today are almost all Muslim, it's reasonable to assume the Antichrist will be a Muslim, as well.

<u>SUPPORT</u>: In Daniel, chapter 2, we learn that all four parts of Nebuchadnezzar's statue will collapse simultaneously when its feet are hit by the "rock cut out without hands." In this scene, Jesus is the "rock," and the four sections of the statue are: Babylon, Medo-Persia, Greece, and the empire of the Antichrist. Obviously, this implies that the first three sections are intrinsically connected to the last, i.e., the empire of the Beast:

> **Daniel 2:34-35** – Thou sawest till that a stone [Jesus] was cut out without hands, which smote the image upon his feet that were of iron and clay, and brake them to pieces. **Then was the iron, the clay, the brass, the silver, and the gold, broken to pieces <u>together</u>,** and became like the chaff of the summer threshing-floors; and the wind carried them away…

Although it might seem difficult to explain how all four empires can be simultaneously destroyed if the first three have been extinct for thousands of years, there's a logical explanation: The Antichrist's dominion will incorporate the same territories that once comprised the empires of Babylon, Medo-Persia, and Greece. And so, the destruction of the Antichrist's empire at Armageddon means the destruction of those other empires, as well.

Consequently, since the countries which now occupy those territories are predominantly Muslim — Iran, Iraq, Greece, and Turkey — it is obvious the Antichrist will rise from one of them as a follower of Islam.

<u>WHY THIS ARGUMENT IS FALSE</u>: Broadly speaking, the picture of Christ destroying all four kingdoms at once signifies that the "world order" which has held sway since the days of Nebuchadnezzar — and which has been dominated by Gentile powers — will be

destroyed by Jesus at his Second Coming. In its place, Jesus will establish a world-wide kingdom of peace and righteousness, under the administrative leadership of Israel (Daniel 2:44).

More narrowly, however, this imagery reveals that Jesus will target the descendants of Greece, Medo-Persia, and Babylon for special punishment at Armageddon. Christ will decimate the progeny of Babylon, Medo-Persia, and Greece, as payment not only for what their ancestors did to the Jews,[41] but for how they themselves have treated God's people, especially over the last seventy years.

However — and this is key — nothing about this imagery indicates that those nations or territories are somehow a part of the Antichrist's kingdom. Nothing about Nebuchadnezzar's statue, its individual com-ponents, or its sudden destruction allows us to infer that the people who now occupy the territories of ancient Babylon, Medo-Persia, and Greece will unite with the Antichrist's final confederacy.

Here's why...

First, the book of Daniel **never states** that Babylon, Medo-Persia, and Greece will be a part of the Antichrist's inner circle. There are no words to the effect: *The first three empires will be a part of the fourth.* Such a conclusion must therefore be reached by inference. It is never explicitly stated in Daniel 2 or anywhere else.

Second, **none of the metals** that were used in the statue to represent Babylon, Medo-Persia, or Greece appear in the statue's legs or feet. In other words, there is no gold, silver, or bronze in the part of the

---

[41] Apparently, Babylon, Medo-Persia, and Greece are being preserved as distinct entities so they may be properly identified and judged at Armageddon. This is confirmed in Daniel 2 by the fact that the metallic components of Nebuchadnezzar's statue are preserved until Jesus (the "rock") comes and destroys them. Daniel 7 then re-verifies this by stating: "As concerning the rest of the beasts [Babylon, Medo-Persia, and Greece], they had their dominion taken away: yet **their lives were prolonged** for a season and time." In other words, the glory and power of these empires were taken away in 539, 331, and 146 B.C. (respectively). Yet their unique people, culture, and borders were (essentially) preserved intact from then until now, so that Christ can identify and repay them at Armageddon for the horrible way they have treated Israel, both as ancient empires and as modern states.

statue that supposedly represents the Antichrist's "amalgamated" empire. Instead, the legs are made of pure iron, while the feet consist of iron and clay.

Third, we know from Revelation 16:14 that **all the nations of the world** will be represented at Armageddon — including the modern states of Iraq, Iran, Turkey, and Greece — and that means all of them will be broken by the Lord at the same instant, *regardless of whether or not they are a part of the Antichrist's inner circle.*

Fourth, the fact that the Beast of Revelation 13 consists of a lion's mouth, a bear's feet, and a leopard's body **does not mean** the Antichrist's empire will consist of the *territories* once held by Nebuchadnezzar, Cyrus, and Alexander. It simply means that the Antichrist *himself* will be more **bold, strong, and clever** than Cyrus, Alexander, and Nebuchadnezzar combined. (See IAT Claim #5.)

Last, but not least, note that at least one of the nations represented in the statue — Greece — **is not Muslim today**. It is 97% Greek Orthodox. In fact, less than 2% of the population is Muslim. Consequently, even if the Antichrist's empire was an amalgamation of the previous three, there are too many non-Muslims in that region to guarantee the Antichrist himself would be a follower of Islam.

Consequently, the sudden destruction of all four parts of Nebuchadnezzar's statue at Armageddon does not prove that Iraq, Iran, Turkey, or Greece *must be* a part of the Antichrist's inner circle, or that the Antichrist *must be* a Muslim, or that he *must come* from Turkey, Greece, Iraq, or Iran.[42] It simply means that Jesus is not going to forget what their ancestors did to his people. Nor is he going to forget what they have done to the Jews over the last 70 years. Instead, all nations — and especially the remnants of Babylon, Medo-Persia, and Greece — are going to be judged and punished when Jesus returns at the Second Coming. And that's why the *entire* statue of Gentile kingdoms will collapse simultaneously.

---

[42] Scholars have confirmed that Iraq, Iran, and Greece are descended from the people of Babylon, Medo-Persia, and ancient Greece (respectively). See, for example, the Wikipedia articles that appear under: "Iranian Peoples," "Iraqis," and "Greeks."

IAT CLAIM #11. The striking similarities between Islamic prophecy and that of the Bible suggest the Antichrist will be a Muslim.

SUPPORT: The resemblance between the end-time prophecies of Scripture and those of Islam is downright eerie. For example, according to Muslims, the Mahdi, like the Antichrist, will:

- Arrive on a white horse

- Broker a seven-year peace treaty

- Hold world-wide political power

- Command an unstoppable military force

- Demand that everyone join his religion or face decapitation

- Possess a special hatred for Christians and Jews

- Attempt to capture Jerusalem

- Try to change societal norms and the order of nations (i.e., he will try to change "times and law")

Clearly, these characteristics — which are nearly identical to those attributed to the Bible's Man of Sin — prove that the Mahdi of Islam and the Antichrist of the Bible are one-and-the-same. The Antichrist must therefore be a Muslim.

WHY THIS ARGUMENT IS FALSE: This notion is wrong on a number of levels. First, it is certain that Islamic eschatology is largely drawn from the prophecies of the the Old Testament and the Apocalypse.[43] This not only explains the similarities between Islamic prophecy and that of the Bible, it also invalidates Islamic eschatology at the outset. Islamic eschatology is not a new and authoritative revelation. It is simply a corrupted version of Old and New Testaments forecasts.

---

[43] See, for example: *The Last Trumpet* (2005) by Dr. Samuel Shahid.

Second, mere similarities between the end-times scenario of the Bible and that of Islam prove nothing, other than that they're similar. In other words, concluding that the Antichrist will be a Muslim, based merely on the fact that the Bible's accounts and those of Islam bear a resemblance is too great a leap of reasoning. They're similar, yes, but only because the details of one have been appropriated by the other, not because they are "separate but complementary" revelations from the same divine source.

In truth, the end-times prophecies of Islam are no more relevant to our discussion than those of Nostradamus or Jeanne Dixon. They tell us what Muslims are expecting. But that's about it. They therefore have no place in a legitimate dialogue concerning the identity and career of the Antichrist.

As Joel Richardson has said:

> And I would never look to Islamic prophecy as if it is actually prophetic... I do not look to it as any source of truth.[44]

Only the Bible contains accurate information in regards to the end-times (Isaiah 46:9-10). It is therefore the exclusive source for determining the truth about future events and personalities. Our understanding of the Antichrist and the Apocalypse must not be colored or informed by Islamic thinking, but guided strictly by the information contained within the sixty-six canonical books of God's Word.[45]

Hence, while the similarities between the Mahdi of Islam and the biblical Antichrist might be amusing, they are similar only because one is a corrupted version of the other. The details concerning the Mahdi do not come from the Holy Spirit and thus are completely powerless to prove *anything* about the Antichrist.

---

[44] https://joelstrumpet.com/?p=5731

[45] Other *false equivalence* arguments should be avoided, as well. These include such dubious notions as the idea that the 'Green Horse' of Revelation 6 signals the 'green flag' of Islam; or the notion that the beheadings in Revelation 6 are tied to the Muslim practice of beheading one's enemies, and so on. These arguments, and others like them, are purely speculative and constitute newspaper exegesis, oversimplification, or false equivalence.

IAT CLAIM #12. The Bible repeatedly refers to the Antichrist by such titles as "the Assyrian" and the "king of Babylon." He must therefore be an Arab from Syria or Iraq.

SUPPORT: The fact that the Bible refers to an end-times warmonger called the *Assyrian* in Isaiah 10:5 and 14:25, and the *King of Babylon* in Isaiah 14:4 and 22, implies that the Antichrist will come from either Assyria or Babylon. On a modern map, those areas correspond to present-day Syria, Turkey, Iraq, and Iran.

Indeed, prophets like Micah seem to confirm this interpretation:

> **Micah 5:5-6** – And this man [the Messiah] shall be the peace, when the **Assyrian** [presumably the Antichrist] shall come into our land [during the Tribulation]: and when he shall tread in our palaces, then shall we raise against him seven shepherds, and eight principal men. And they shall waste the land of Assyria with the sword... thus shall he [the Messiah] deliver us from the **Assyrian**, when he cometh into our land...

WHY THIS ARGUMENT IS FALSE: Several facts make it doubtful these verses are saying the Antichrist is either Assyrian or Babylonian. First, since Babylon and Assyria were two separate kingdoms, with two different homelands, two different capitals, two different languages (dialects), two different cultures, two different ethnicities, and two different dynasties, it is impossible that both titles (*the Assyrian* and *the King of Babylon*) could be referring to the Antichrist's ethnicity or point of origin. If they did, then a major contradiction would exist because it would require the Antichrist to be born in both Syria and Iraq (the modern geographic equivalents of Assyria and Babylon), which of course is not possible.

Second, none of the passages which are typically cited in support of the *Assyrian Antichrist theory* or the *Babylonian Antichrist theory* explicitly say the passage is speaking about the Antichrist. Consequently, the identity of the central character in those passages is up for debate. For example:

> **Isaiah 10:5-6** – O **Assyrian**, the rod of mine anger, and
> the staff in their hand is mine indignation. I will send him
> against an hypocritical nation [Israel], and against the
> people of my wrath will I give him a charge, to take the
> spoil, and to take the prey, and to tread them down like
> the mire of the streets.

Is the prophet speaking about the end times, or is he simply warning
the people of his own time that God is about to use the king of Assyria
to punish Israel for its transgressions? It's hard to say. According to
many expositors, the punishment that Isaiah predicts in the above
verses was fulfilled by Shalmaneser in 722 B.C., and whether or not
there will be a second fulfillment by the Antichrist is far from certain.

* * * *

> **Micah 5:5-6** – And this man [the Messiah] shall be the
> peace, when the **Assyrian** shall come into our land: and
> when he shall tread in our palaces, then shall we raise
> against him [the Assyrian] seven shepherds, and eight
> principal men. And they shall waste the land of Assyria
> with the sword, and the land of Nimrod in the entrances
> thereof: thus shall he [the Messiah] deliver us from the
> **Assyrian**, when he cometh into our land, and when he
> treadeth within our borders.

In this case, the prophet definitely appears to be speaking about the
end times. We can make this assessment because Israel never van-
quished Assyria in the manner described. That conquest is still in the
future. But is Micah prophesying about the Antichrist, or is he
speaking about one of the doomed Arab leaders who will line up
against Israel at the Battle of Armageddon? Could the prophet simply
be talking about a man like Bashar Al-Assad, the current leader of
Syria, and not the Antichrist? The text appears to contain no defin-
itive statement either way, which means the notion of an Assyrian
Antichrist has been inferred from text, not read from the text.

* * * *

Isaiah 14:3-7, 20-23 – It shall come to pass in the day the Lord gives you [Israel] rest from your sorrow…that you will take up this proverb against the **king of Babylon**, and say: 'How the oppressor has ceased, The golden city ceased! The Lord has broken the staff of the wicked, The scepter of the rulers; He who struck the people in wrath with a continual stroke, He who ruled the nations in anger, Is persecuted and no one hinders. The whole earth is at rest and quiet…' 'They that see thee shall narrowly look upon thee, and consider thee, saying, Is this the man that made the earth to tremble, that did shake kingdoms; That made the world as a wilderness, and destroyed the cities thereof; that opened not the house of his prisoners?' …For I will rise up against them,' says the Lord of hosts, 'And cut off from **Babylon** the name and remnant, and offspring and posterity,' says the Lord. 'I will also make it a possession for the porcupine, and marshes of muddy water; I will sweep it with the broom of destruction,' says the Lord of hosts.

The King of Babylon in this passage is almost certainly the Antichrist. The evidence for this includes the fact that no king has ever "made the world as a wilderness, and destroyed the cities thereof," nor was ancient Babylon ever "swept with the broom of destruction," nor has the "whole earth" ever been "at rest."

But is the prophet speaking of *literal* Babylon, or is he using a codeword for *another* metropolis whose sin and idolatry rival that of the ancient capital…*but which lies entirely outside of Arabia?*

Let us not forget that John the apostle also spoke about an end-times "Babylon" and its king. And both he and Isaiah seem to be talking about the same city. But John was more descriptive than Isaiah and revealed that this end-times "Babylon" was the center of military, commercial, and spiritual power in 95 A.D.:

Revelation 17:18 – And the woman [Mystery Babylon] whom you saw **is** that great city which **reigns** over the kings of the earth. [Note the present tense of this verse.]

In my opinion, the only city that fits this description is Rome. One might disagree with that assessment and propose some other city, but even so, one still could not propose *literal* Babylon as a possible candidate, because in John's day *literal* Babylon was nothing but an insignificant outpost in the middle of a desert. It was a shadow of its former self. It was not the center of military, commercial, or spiritual power in 95 A.D., as John specified in his prophecy.

Consequently, Isaiah's passage concerning the "king of Babylon" cannot be saying the Antichrist will come from *literal* Babylon. And that means the text cannot be used to prove the Antichrist will come from a rebuilt Babylon in modern Iraq, or from any other part of Arabia.[46]

* * * *

> **Ezekiel 28:1-5** – The word of the Lord came again unto me, saying, "Son of man, say unto the **prince of Tyrus**, Thus saith the Lord God; Because thine heart is lifted up, and thou hast said, I am a God, I sit in the seat of God, in the midst of the seas; yet thou art a man, and not God, though thou set thine heart as the heart of God…"

If Ezekiel is talking about the Antichrist in the verses above — and it appears that he is, because the Antichrist is the only man in history who will have the audacity to "sit in the seat of God" — then the idea of an *Islamic* Antichrist becomes even more muddied, especially if these titles are taken as geographic markers: Is the Antichrist now from Assyria, Babylon…or perhaps Tyre?

* * * *

In short, when it comes to the texts that allegedly prove the Antichrist is the king of Assyria, Babylon, or some other Middle East nation,

---

[46] In my view, the evidence of Scripture proves decisively that the Antichrist is a Roman. Please see *Empire of the Antichrist* and *The Antichrist* (Positron Books).

none of those passages explicitly make such a statement, many of those verses seem to contradict each other (if we assume they're speaking about the Antichrist's birthplace), and it's not always clear which ones are speaking about the last days and which are speaking about events that have already happened. For these reasons, it is unreasonable to conclude that the Antichrist is ethnically Assyrian, Babylonian, or otherwise "Arabic," based on the above prophecies.

Indeed, the ambiguity of these scriptures explains why there is no consensus among IAT proponents as to the Antichrist's actual point of origin. Some say it's Turkey, others say Syria, several more say Iraq, a few believe Persia (Iran), a handful say Greece or Jordan, and still others claim Lebanon or Saudi Arabia. No one is sure. And few IAT expositors are willing to take a stand on this particular question. (And we haven't even touched on the theory that the Antichrist is Russian, by virtue of Ezekiel's prophecy regarding a monarch called "Gog.")

In truth, these texts are so inconclusive that some scholars theorize the titles *the Assyrian* and *King of Babylon* might even refer to the pope or Satan!

That's quite a stretch, in my opinion. But the point is that all of these passages are so foggy that not even the brightest commentators are sure as to whom *the Assyrian* and *King of Babylon* might be *if* we assume those titles are meant to indicate the nationality of the Antichrist, or his geographic point of origin.

Therefore, from my perspective, the proper way to assess the preceding titles in relation to the Antichrist (King of Babylon, King of Assyria, Prince of Tyre, etc.) is not to see them as indicators of the Antichrist's bloodline or citizenship, but to see them as *historical archetypes*, each of whom provides some insight into the Antichrist's bloodthirsty personality and his anti-Semitic goals — not his ethnicity or national origin.[47]

---

[47] I do believe, however, that the name "Gog" points to the Antichrist's patriarchal lineage (Genesis 10). Please see my upcoming book, *Gog of Magog,* for a full explanation.

IAT CLAIM #13. Although Muslims will never follow a man who claims to be God or demands to be worshipped, Muslims could support an Islamic Antichrist because he won't actually claim to be "God," nor will he require any Muslim to actually "worship" him.

<u>SUPPORT</u>: It is clear from the writings of Islam that the Muslim community will never embrace a man who claims to be God. Therefore, even though 2 Thessalonians 2:4 says the Antichrist will enter the Temple in Jerusalem and make some pretty outrageous claims, those claims will not amount to a declaration of divinity.

Indeed, the Antichrist will not claim to be God, or even *a* god. Instead, he will simply declare himself to be superior to *Jehovah*, that is, above the God of the Jews. That is something most Muslims could live with and might even welcome.

Further, the phrase, "and they worshipped the beast," in Revelation 13, doesn't mean that Muslims will actually worship the Antichrist. It simply means that Muslims will give him their utmost admiration and respect. In other words, the word "worship," in this case, doesn't imply the kind of adoration reserved exclusively for God. Instead, it merely implies a high level of esteem, veneration, or obedience.

Thus, the Antichrist could be a Muslim because he won't actually claim to be God or require the people of Islam to worship him.

<u>WHY THIS ARGUMENT IS FALSE</u>: This argument consists of two parts, both of which are irretrievably flawed. Let's start by examining the claim that Muslims won't actually worship the Beast:

1. According to John the apostle, *all* the people of earth will worship both Lucifer (the Dragon) and the Antichrist (the Beast) as soon as the Man of Sin steps onto the world stage, *including* Muslims. The relevant verses in the Apocalypse could hardly be more clear:

   > **Revelation13:4** — And they **worshipped** the dragon which gave power unto the beast: and they **worshipped** the beast, saying, Who is like unto the beast? who is able to make war with him?

Revelation 13:8 — And **all that dwell** upon the earth **shall worship** him [the Antichrist], whose names are not written in the book of life of the Lamb slain from the foundation of the world.

The plain teaching of these verses is that "all who dwell upon the earth" — i.e., every person who is not a follower of Christ — will voluntarily worship the devil and the Antichrist at some point during the Tribulation. And that necessarily includes Muslims, because no exceptions are listed.

Of course, John's prediction does seem like a paradox: How could people of so many different backgrounds — including Jews, Buddhists, Catholics, Hindus, Atheists, and *especially* Muslims — suddenly start worshipping the Beast and the Dragon?

The solution, according to those who support the IAT, is to realize that the word "worship" in the above passage does not refer to the kind of worship that's reserved for deity. Instead, it refers to the kind of honor and deference that's paid to a highly esteemed individual, such as a president or a religious leader:

> The word used here for "worship" is the Greek *proskyneō* … So while *proskyneō* most often refers to "worship," as to God or to a god, **it does not exclusively mean this**. The *Theological Dictionary of the New Testament* defines the Jewish understanding of *proskyneō* as: "the term for various words meaning 'to bow,' 'to kiss,' 'to serve,' and 'to worship.' …Most of the instances relate to veneration of the God of Israel or false gods. [But it] may also be directed to angels, to the righteous, to rulers, [and] to the prophets…"[48] [Boldface added.]

That might sound like a reasonable explanation. But it fails to account for one critical truth: John never would've emphasized the fact that people everywhere will "worship" these two evil persons *unless* that worship constituted something extraordinarily wicked,

---

[48] Joel Richardson, *Mideast Beast* (Wash., D.C.: WND Books, 2012), p. 134-135.

i.e., something that was a major transgression in the eyes of the Lord. Notice that John highlights this worship not once, but three times, and he ties it exclusively to unsaved people, i.e., "those who dwell upon the earth," a technical phrase that always refers to people who have rejected Christ as God and Savior.

The real question, therefore, is not whether the "worship" of those who dwell upon the earth constitutes actual worship — it does — but how it's possible for people of so many differing backgrounds, including pagans, Jews, Buddhists, Hindus, nominal Christians, Catholics, atheists, *and especially* Muslims, to suddenly start worshipping the Beast and the Dragon.

In my opinion the correct answer, as opposed to the one offered by IAT proponents, lies not in a special definition of the word "worship," but in the realization that this particular act of worship in Revelation 13 is being assessed from God's point of view, not man's. In other words, Muslims and other people who "dwell upon the earth" might not consider their adoration of the Antichrist to be idolatry or "worship," but God absolutely will.[49]

Consequently, when John says that people everywhere will worship the Beast and the Dragon, that's exactly what he means. All mankind — including Muslims — will really and truly worship the Beast and his father, the devil. And they will do this by uttering one simple phrase: "Who is like the Beast? Who is able to make war with him?" That is the worship John is talking about:

> **Revelation 13:4** – And they **worshipped** the dragon which gave power unto the beast: and they **worshipped** the beast, **saying**, Who is like unto the beast? who is able to make war with him?

---

[49] Remember, Jesus said that the way *we* see our sins isn't always how *God* sees them. We humans tend to take a much lighter (or even non-existent) view of our transgressions. We don't think that putting wealth above God is idolatry. We don't see hate as murder, or lust as adultery. Yet that's precisely how God sees these things (Mt. 5:21-28; 19:22).

All who repeat this phrase will be violating the Second Commandment and genuinely worshipping the Antichrist. The catch is that most people, including those in the Muslim community, will not perceive this utterance as a violation of God's Law.[50] They will not think of this perverse doxology as "worship," but God definitely will.

Again, the argument promoted by those who support the Islamic Antichrist Theory relies on a special definition of the word "worship," which (in my view) is not very satisfying:

> In summary, then, in light of the range of meaning of *proskyneō*, we must be cautious in declaring dogmatically that the Antichrist will be worshipped as God or a god. **These verses in Revelation 13 that state that the Antichrist will receive worship could simply indicate that the people of the earth will display utter submission to him...**[51] [Boldface added.]

It is true that the term "worship" (*proskyneō*) can refer to a simple act of respect or submission. However, we know that the word "worship" in Revelation 13 signifies the kind of adoration reserved for God alone, because the very refrain, *Who is like unto the beast? Who can make war with him?* constitutes a perverse doxology, that has been lifted straight out of the psalms that glorify God. In other words, the praise of the Antichrist recorded in Revelation 13 is patterned after the sacred praises of God, and it attributes to the Antichrist characteristics that are reserved exclusively to the Most High:

- **Jeremiah 49:19** – For **who is like Me**, and who will summon Me into court? And who then is the shepherd **who can stand against Me**?

- **Psalm 35:10** – **LORD, who is like You**, Who delivers the afflicted from him **who is too strong for him**...?

---

[50] People will be especially blind to the perversity of their worship after God sends a powerful "delusion" that will cause them to believe the deceptions of the enemy (2 Thess. 2:11).

[51] Joel Richardson, *Mideast Beast* (Wash., D.C.: WND Books, 2012), p. 134-135.

- **Exodus 15:11 – Who is like You** among the gods, O LORD? Who is like You, majestic in holiness, Awesome in praises, **working wonders**?

- **Psalm 113:5 – Who is like the LORD our God**, Who is **enthroned on high...**

- **Pslam 89:6** – For **who in the heaven can be compared unto the Lord**? who among the sons of the mighty [i.e., who among the angels] can be **likened unto the Lord**?

Get the picture?

Consequently, by simply reciting the doxology of Revelation 13:4, Muslims will be worshipping the Antichrist and Satan, whether they realize it or not. They will be violating the Second Commandment *from God's point of view*. And that's the view that counts.[52]

To repeat: Muslims might not outright pray to the Beast, or think of him as Allah. But in violation of the Second Commandment they will *proskyneō* the Antichrist to a degree far in excess of mere "reverence," "respect," or "submission."

In effect, they will be declaring the Antichrist and his father, the devil, to be both divine ("Who is like you?") and invincible ("Who can make war with you?"), thus attributing to the Beast and the Dragon traits that belong exclusively to the Almighty. The Islamic community, and the rest of mankind, might not consider their praise of the Antichrist to be sacrilegious worship, but God surely will.[53]

---

[52] That the doxology in Revelation 13 constitutes actual worship of the Antichrist is further supported by the fact that Tribulation saints do not take part in it (implied by v. 7-8).

[53] In my view, the Muslim worship of Antichrist will occur only during the first half of the Tribulation, that is, while the Muslim community still believes he is their ally against Israel. However, the moment the Antichrist enters the Temple in Jerusalem and claims to be God, the nations of Islam will be totally outraged. They will reject the Antichrist and fight him for control of the Holy Land. This will lead to the wars and mayhem of the second half of the Tribulation.

2. That brings us to the second question: Will the Antichrist actually claim to be God when he sits in the rebuilt Temple in Jerusalem? Proponents of the Islamic Antichrist Theory say no. The Antichrist might sit in the Temple and receive the adoration of mankind, but he will never actually say the words, "I am God." No Muslim would ever say such a thing, and no person who did would ever be embraced by the Muslim community.

Therefore, according to those who support the IAT, when Paul says the Antichrist will "as God, sit in the temple of God, showing himself that he is God," he does not mean that the Beast will declare himself to be God. Instead, he means that the Antichrist, as a Muslim, will mock the God of Israel and claim to be superior to Him.

In my opinion, this interpretation certainly has the advantage of being original. But it also fails to account for several key scriptures which indicate that the Antichrist will do certain things no Muslim would even contemplate. Consider these statements:

- **2 Thessalonians 2:4** — [The Antichrist] **as God** sitteth in the temple of God, **shewing himself that he is God**.

- **Daniel 8:11** — **He even exalted himself as high as the Prince of the host** [i.e., Jesus]; and by him the daily sacrifices were taken away, and the place of His sanctuary was cast down.

- **Revelation 13:15** — [The False Prophet required] that **as many as would not worship the image of the beast should be killed**.

- **2 Thessalonians 2:3-4** — [A]nd that man of sin...[will] **exalteth himself above all that is called God**.

Let me ask the reader: Would a Muslim show himself to be God? Would a Muslim force people to worship his image? Would a Muslim declare himself to be higher than *all* that is called God? Of course not! Yet, that's exactly what these verses declare. While none of them explicitly say the Antichrist will announce to the world, "I am God," the combined effect of these statements is that the Antichrist will do just that.[54]

The fact that Scripture doesn't record that particular line of blasphemy is academic. It's a distinction without a difference, because even Daniel said the Antichrist would declare himself to be higher than every other god, *including* Allah:

> **Daniel 11:36-37** – [A]nd he [the Antichrist] shall exalt himself, and **magnify himself above every god**, and shall speak marvellous things against the God of gods… **Neither shall he…regard any god: for he shall magnify himself above all**.

Daniel is clear. At some point during the Tribulation, the Antichrist will disrespect every god, and will magnify himself above every god, including Allah. These are things no Muslim would do. Indeed, these antics will shock and offend the Muslim community so deeply, that the entire Islamic nation will turn on the Antichrist and take up arms against him during the last half of the Tribulation. (Please see IAT Claim #14.)

Indeed, it is hard to imagine a more explicit set of statements that could communicate the idea that the Antichrist, as the devil's representative, will claim to hold the office of the Almighty. After all, taking Christ's place as the God of the universe has been Satan's goal from time immemorial. Why would he change it now?

> **Isaiah 14:12-14** – How you are fallen from heaven, O Lucifer, son of the morning! *How* you are cut down to the ground, You who weakened the nations! For you have said in your heart: "I will ascend into heaven, I will exalt my throne above the stars of God; I will also sit on the mount of the congregation On the farthest sides of the north; I will ascend above the heights of the clouds, **I will be like the Most High**."

---

[54] Ezekiel 28:1-10 also implies, by way of historical type, that the Antichrist will actually claim to be God: "Because thine heart is lifted up, and **thou hast said, I am a God, I sit in the seat of God**, in the midst of the seas; yet thou art a man, and not God…"

Clearly, as Satan's ambassador, the Antichrist will echo Lucifer's insatiable desire to be worshipped and will claim to hold the title of the "Most High."

Therefore, since the Antichrist will claim to be God in the flesh — thereby violating one of the greatest tenets of Islam — we are left with only one conclusion: The Antichrist cannot be a Muslim.

IAT CLAIM #14. Ezekiel 38 says that the Antichrist—known in this chapter as "Gog"—will lead a group of *Muslim nations* to the Battle of Armageddon. Therefore, the Antichrist must be a Muslim.

SUPPORT: According to Ezekiel 38, a very specific alliance of nations will march against Israel at the time of the end. Those nations include Togarmah, Gomer, Persia, Ethiopia, and Libya. Today, these territories roughly include the nations of Turkey, Iran, Sudan, and Libya. Together they form a hostile "outer ring" around Israel. And nearly all of the people in those countries are Muslim.

Moreover, the Antichrist — whom Ezekiel calls "Gog" in this chapter[55] — is predicted to take charge of these forces and lead them on an invasion of the Holy Land which will end at Armageddon:

> **Ezekiel 38:7, 9, 18, 21** – Be thou prepared [Gog], and prepare for thyself, thou, and **all thy company that are assembled unto thee**, and be thou a **guard** unto them... Thou shalt ascend and come like a storm, thou shalt be like a cloud to cover the land [of Israel], thou, and **all thy bands**, and **many people with thee**... And it shall come to pass at the same time when Gog shall come against the land of Israel, saith the Lord God, that my fury shall come up in my face... And I will call for a sword against him [Gog] throughout all my mountains...

---

[55] Please see my book, *Gog of Magog,* for an explanation of the title, "Gog of Magog, chief prince of Meshech and Tubal." This refers to the Antichrist's bloodline, not to the nations he will command.

Obviously, the Antichrist — or "Gog" — is the man who will lead these nations to Armageddon. And since most of these nations are Muslim, the Antichrist must be a Muslim, as well.

WHY THIS ARGUMENT IS FALSE: Gog is indeed the Antichrist in this narrative. And the nations listed as Togarmah, Gomer, Persia, Ethiopia (Cush), and Libya (Put) are undoubtedly Turkey, Iran, Sudan, and parts of present-day Libya and Algeria. All of them are thoroughly Muslim.

However, despite what many expositors believe, Ezekiel 38:7 does not say that Gog will be the leader, king, commander, president, comrade, emperor, caliph, or ally of those nations. It says he will be their "**imprisoner**" or "**jailer**." That is the meaning of the relevant text:

> Be thou prepared [Gog], and prepare for thyself, thou, and all thy company that are assembled unto thee, and be thou a **guard** [imprisoner] unto them...

The critical word in this narrative is *mishmar*. The King James Version translates *mishmar* as "guard." Other Bibles translate it (here) as "lookout," "commander," or "leader." However, the actual term means warden, jailer, detention officer, bailiff, prison guard, jail cell, dungeon, or penitentiary. It never means anything else.[56]

Consequently, verse 38:7 does not teach that the Antichrist will lead the Muslim nations on their march to Israel, or that he will fight alongside them at the Battle of Armageddon. Instead, it teaches that the Antichrist will act as their *jailer*. He will pull all these people to their destruction and subsequent internment in hell. He will goad these nations into a fight at Megiddo, and thus lead them to God's slaughter, the way a prison guard leads convicted felons to their execution.

---

[56] On occasion *mishmar* can also mean "protector," but that's not the sense indicated here. The Antichrist isn't protecting these groups from anyone. In fact, the Septuagint version of v. 38:7 shows that the Greek translators understood Gog to be performing a "service" for the Almighty: "[A]nd thou [Gog] shalt be to me for a guard." In other words, if I may paraphrase, *And you, O Gog, shall serve me as a **prison guard**. You will be my **bailiff**. You will summon all of my enemies to the Valley of Jehoshaphat so that I may judge and incarcerate all of them at once.*

Indeed, Isaiah used this very terminology to describe that event:

> **Isaiah 24:22** — And they [the nations of the earth] shall be gathered together, as **prisoners** are gathered in the pit, and shall be shut up in the **prison** [of hell]...

Revelation 16:13-14 completes the picture:

> And I saw **three unclean spirits**...come out of the mouth of **the dragon** [Satan], and out of the mouth of **the beast** [Gog, the Antichrist], and out of the mouth of **the false prophet**. For they are the spirits of devils, working **miracles**, which go forth unto the kings of the earth and of the whole world, **to gather them to the battle of that great day of God Almighty**.

In other words, as the final showdown draws near, the Antichrist — along with the Dragon and the False Prophet — will send their demonic emissaries to pull the nations mentioned in Ezekiel 38 to the Battle of Armageddon.[57] They will pull them into the prison of hell.

In practical terms, this likely means the Antichrist and the False Prophet will provoke the international community with acrimonious insults and outrageous demands. Both of these men will insist that the Antichrist is still God on earth and that anyone who disobeys him will face his wrath. Spurred by Satan's thirst for total control, the Antichrist will "assemble to himself" the kings of the Middle East, and goad them into a battle where (he believes) he can smash the nations who resist his authority, once and for all.

Unaware that God is manipulating their words and actions for his own purposes, the Antichrist and the False Prophet will incite Iran, Sudan, Turkey, and the rest of the Muslim countries which form Ezekiel's "outer ring," to march to the Mountains of Megiddo so that the entire lot can be destroyed in one fell swoop — only it will be *God Almighty*

---

[57] In the Old Testament, God says he will draw all nations to Israel for the final showdown (Joel 3:2, 11; Zech. 14:1-3; Zeph. 3:8; Ez. 38:4-9). In the Apocalypse, God then reveals how he intends to do that: It will be through the taunts of Satan, the Antichrist, and the False Prophet, combined with the encouragement of three hideous demons (Rev. 16:14, 16).

who will be doing the destroying:

> **Ezekiel 38:14-23** – Therefore, son of man, prophesy and say to **Gog** [the Antichrist]… "It will be in the latter days that **I will bring you against My land**, so that the nations may know Me, when I am hallowed in you, O Gog, before their eyes…" And I will bring him [Gog, the Antichrist] to judgment with pestilence and bloodshed; I will rain down on him, on **his troops** [i.e., the new-Roman forces of Europe], and on the **many peoples who *are* with him** [i.e., all the other nations that have been drawn to Armageddon, including the Muslim kingdoms], flooding rain, great hailstones, fire, and brimstone. **Thus I will magnify Myself and sanctify Myself, and I will be known in the eyes of many nations**. Then they shall know that I *am* the Lord.

In short, God will use the Antichrist as bait to draw the armies of Islam to their doom at Armageddon. The Muslims will be "with" the Antichrist, but only in the sense of their being in the same place (Israel), at the same time (at the end of the Tribulation). It will not be in the sense of their being allies or comrades, or having the same purpose. In fact, far from being friends of the Antichrist, the nations of Islam will be absolutely outraged by the Antichrist's claim to be higher than Allah (Dan. 11:37). And that means the Antichrist will be the *enemy* of the Muslims at the Battle of Armageddon, not their kinsman or leader.

Indeed, the animosity that will exist between the Antichrist and the Islamic nations is plainly stated in Daniel 11 and Ezekiel 38:

> **Daniel 11:40** — And at the time of the end shall the king of the south [**Egypt, Libya, Algeria, Tunisia**] push at him [the Antichrist]: and the king of the north [the Antichrist] shall come against him [the king of the south] like a whirlwind, with chariots, and with horsemen, and with many ships; and he shall enter into the countries, and shall overflow and pass over.

> **Daniel 11:41-43** — He [the Antichrist] shall enter also into the glorious land [Israel], and many countries [in the

Middle East] shall be overthrown [by the Antichrist]: but these shall escape out of his hand, even **Edom** [south Jordan], and **Moab** [central Jordan], and the chief of the children of **Ammon** [north Jordan]. He shall stretch forth his hand also upon the countries: and the land of **Egypt** shall not escape. But he shall have power over the treasures of gold and of silver, and over all the precious things of **Egypt**: and the **Libyans** [North Africa] and the **Ethiopians** [central Sudan] shall be at his steps.

Daniel 11:44-45 — But tidings out of the east [most likely **Iraq**, **Iran**, and **Saudi Arabia**, among others] and out of the north [most likely **Syria**, **Lebanon**, and **Turkey**, among others] shall trouble him [the Antichrist]: therefore he shall go forth with great fury to destroy, and utterly to make away many... Yet he shall come to his end, and none shall help him.

Ezekiel 38:13 — Sheba [**Ethiopia** and/or **Yemen**], and Dedan [**Saudi Arabia**], and the merchants of Tarshish [possibly **Lebanon** or **Tunisia**], with all the young lions thereof, shall say unto thee, Art thou come to take a spoil? hast thou gathered thy company to take a prey? to carry away silver and gold, to take away cattle and goods, to take a great spoil?

To put it plainly, the Antichrist is not from Turkey, Iran, or any part of Arabia. He is not a Muslim warrior or a friend of the Islamic community. Instead, after he commits the Abomination of Desolation, he will be seen as their bitter enemy. The Antichrist therefore cannot be a Muslim.

The chart below, which is based on the preceding scriptures, makes it clear that almost every Muslim nation in the vicinity of Israel will act as an *opponent* of the Antichrist at Armageddon, thus proving he cannot be their leader, general, caliph, compatriot, or commander. Instead, the Antichrist will be their mortal enemy. And that means the Antichrist, himself, cannot be a Muslim.

Muslim nations will hate the Antichrist and be drawn to Armageddon to fight him (Dan. 11 and Ezek. 38)

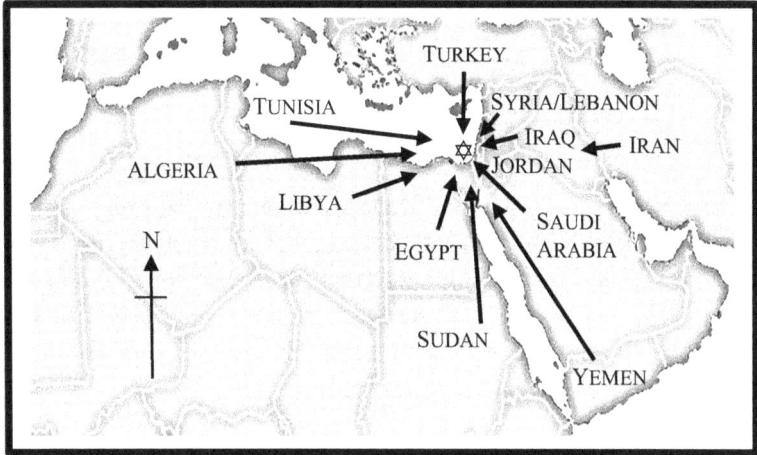

IAT CLAIM #15. The prophecies of Daniel indicate that a powerful king will soon rise in Turkey and attack the country of Iran. In the aftermath of that war, four Islamic kingdoms will be created. Then, out of one of those kingdoms, an Islamic Antichrist will arise and subdue the entire planet.

<u>SUPPORT</u>: In Daniel 8, the he-Goat seems to represent the modern nation of Turkey and its authoritarian leader, Recep Erdogan. Erdogan is one of the most powerful leaders Turkey has ever known, and he is desperate to re-establish the Islamic Caliphate (or perhaps the Ottoman Empire). Recently, he has been at odds with Israel and the West.

However, his true impediment to the throne of Islam is Iran, a nation whose leaders belong to a rival sect of the Muslim community. In the very near future, therefore, Erdogan will order his military forces to charge eastward and conquer Iran, using a devastating blitzkrieg attack. He will smash the Ayatollahs in one, all-out push!

According to Daniel:

Daniel 8:5-6 – And as I was considering, behold, an he goat [presumably Turkey] came from the west [i.e., charged towards the east]... and touched not the ground: and the goat had a notable horn between his eyes [presumably Erdogan]. And he came to the ram that had two horns [presumably Iran]...and ran unto him in the fury of his power.

In the wake of this war, four Islamic kingdoms (the "four notable ones" of verses 8 and 22) will be established. Their territory will encompass and (essentially) match that of the ancient Islamic Caliphate. Then, out of one of those four kingdoms, the Antichrist will rise as the "little horn" of verses 9 and 23, and take over the entire Near East and Mediterranean coastlands.

Daniel 8:8-9 – Therefore the he goat [presumably, the leader of Turkey] waxed very great: and when he was strong, the great horn was broken; and for it came up four notable ones [supposedly four new Muslim kingdoms] toward the four winds of heaven. And out of one of them came forth a little horn [the Antichrist], which waxed exceeding great, toward the south, and toward the east, and toward the pleasant land.

All of this is suppported by the fact that the Angel (who explains the vision) seems to place all the characters and events of chapter 8 in the end times:

- **Daniel 8:17** (NASB) – Son of man, understand that **the vision pertains to the time of the end**.

- **Daniel 8:19** (KJV) – Behold, I will make thee know **what shall be in the last end** of the indignation.

- **Daniel 8:23** (NIV) – **In the latter part of their reign**, when rebels have become completely wicked, a fierce-looking king, a master of intrigue, will arise.

Clearly, the Ram, the Goat, the Four Notable Ones, and the Little Horn are not historical figures like Alexander the Great, or Antiochus IV, or Seleucus, but future personalities who will rise in the Middle East "at the time of the end." They are therefore bound to be Muslims.

WHY THIS ARGUMENT IS FALSE: This interpretation of Daniel 8 is deeply flawed:

1. First, a plain reading of Daniel 8 shows that verses 5-8 and 21-22 *do not* pertain to some future Islamic kingdom, but to **Alexander the Great** and the generals who divided his empire after he died. The details of Alexander's well-known career match virtually every element in Daniel's narrative with stunning precision:

   - In accordance with verses 5 and 21, Alexander was the first king of Grecia.[58]

   - In accordance with verses 5 and 7, Alexander raced east-ward across the known world (that is, the world known to the Jews) and was absolutely invincible.

   - In accordance with verses 6 and 7, Alexander defeated the Medo-Persian empire and brought that kingdom under his control. (The Angel specifically identifies the "ram" as the kingdom of "Media and Persia" in verse 20.)

---

[58] Historians agree that Alexander was the "first king" of a united Greek hegemon, just as Daniel foretold. In fact, the Greek city-states were not unified under one ruler until Alexander pressed the city of Sparta in 331 B.C. (See, for example, the Wikipedia article, "League of Corinth.") Thus, despite the musings of some IAT proponents, neither Phillip of Macedon (Alexander's father), nor any other leader besides Alexander the Great, qualifies as the "first king of Grecia," in the sense indicated by Daniel's prophecy. [**Note**: The original Hebrew doesn't actually say "Grecia." It says *Javan*. But due to a common ancestry (Javan was the patriarch of the people who settled western Turkey and Ionia Greece), this term can refer to the people of ancient Greece or Asia Minor, depending on context. Writers from that era, such as Josephus, verify this convention. (See *Antiquities of the Jews*, Book 1, Chap. 6, Para. 1.) Furthermore, it is indisputable that Alexander was the first-and-only king of the Greeks to race eastward and conquer more territory than any man in history (vv. 5 and 7). And finally, while Alexander himself was Macedonian, he was nevertheless king of the people of Grecia, which is all that the words of the prophecy require.]

- In accordance with verse 8, Alexander died suddenly at the height of his power.

- In accordance with verses 8 and 22 (and Daniel 11:4), none of Alexander's kinsmen inherited his empire. Instead, several of Alexander's top generals claimed the empire and then divided it into **four** territories which they kept for themselves.

- In accordance with verse 22, the combined territory of these generals fell short of the total area that had been under Alexander's control, and none of these generals was ever as politically powerful or successful in battle as Alexander.

- Significantly, almost every secular scholar who has studied this era[59] (i.e., historians who have no axe to grind on the subject of Daniel 8) says that **four** of Daniel's successors — whom scholars have actually labeled the *Diadochi*, literally, the Successors — eventually divided his empire into **four** major regions, thereby setting the stage for the Hellenistic Period and world events for the next 300 years.

2. Next, as previously demonstrated in this essay, Daniel 8:9 places the Antichrist's homeland to the **northwest** of Israel — a fact that immediately rules out Turkey (which lies to the north of Judaea), along with virtually every nation whose territory was formerly a part of the Greek, Medo-Persian, and Babylonian empires. Why? Because, aside from the Greek homeland itself, none of those territories were located northwest of Israel.[60] (Please see the map on page 37.)

---

[59] See, for example, *Dividing the Spoils*, by Robin Waterfield (2011), and *The Wars of Alexander's Successors 323-281 B.C.*, by Bob Bennett and Mike Roberts (2008).

[60] I suppose one could argue that the territory now corresponding to Albania and North Macedonia was once a part of Alexander's empire, and that 49% of the corresponding population is now Muslim. However, that is offset by the fact that the governments of both countries are secular, over 50% of the total population is *not* Muslim, and Albanians and

3. Next, given the political realities of today's Middle East, the idea that four new Islamic governments will suddenly pop into being in the aftermath of a war and take over the territory that once comprised the old Islamic Caliphate (or even the Ottoman Empire) is extremely hard to believe. The disparity that exists between the 20-odd nations that now occupy this territory — in terms of their relative size, wealth, military strength, religious toleration, and politics (not to mention the fractious nature of Arab society, in general) — makes such a rearrangement extremely unlikely.

Although certain pan-Arabic agencies do exist, such as the Arab League, the Islamic Brotherhood, and OPEC, none of these organizations exercise political control over their members. Instead, these entities serve merely as forums to set common goals, discuss ways and means, and settle disagreements among members. They are not governmental or sovereign in nature.

4. Finally, Daniel 8 does not teach that the Ram, the Goat, and the Four Horns will arise in the near future. Instead, the narrative teaches that these kingdoms *have already come and gone*. They therefore cannot be the entities that will produce the future Antichrist.

Let me repeat that: According to the Scriptures, the Ram, the Goat, and the Four Notable Ones are historical empires which have long since passed. They are not coming back. Instead, they're separated from the upcoming "little horn" by almost 2500 years.

We know these three empires belong to the past — and not the future — for three simple reasons:

North Macedonians are not Arabs (i.e., they're not descended from the ancient tribes that were located around Israel.)

a. **The Ram, the Goat, and the Four Horns are placed in the historical era, not in the end times.**

The chronological construction of chapter 8 is very clear on this:

Historical Era – Ram, Goat, and Four Notable Ones (v. 20-22): "The ram which thou sawest having two horns are the kings of Media and Persia. And the rough goat is the king of Grecia: and the great horn that is between his eyes is the first king. Now that being broken, whereas four [notable ones] stood up for it, four kingdoms shall stand up out of the nation, but not in his power."

Chronological break (v. 23; NIV): "In the latter part of their reign, when rebels have become completely wicked..."

Final Era – Little Horn (v. 23): "[A] king of fierce countenance (the Antichrist)...shall stand up.

Clearly the Little Horn — and he alone — is the one who will "stand up" in the last days, that is, when mankind has become "completely wicked."

The first two empires, on the other hand — the goat and the ram — are relegated to the past. They are specifically excluded from the "latter days" segment of this prophecy. In fact, in verses 20 and 21, the Angel explicitly tells Daniel the Ram is the Medo-Persian empire, and the Goat is the Grecian empire. These were historical dynasties. They ended in 331 B.C. and 63 B.C., respectively. Consequently, there is no chance these kingdoms are a part of the events of the last-days.

This evidence *alone* means the Antichrist is not about to rise from Greece, Medo-Persia (Iran), or even a four-part caliphate, because according to verse 23, the Medo-Persians, the Greeks, and the Four Notable Ones (whatever they were) existed centuries ago. They came and went eons before our own time. But that's not all...

b. **While everything mentioned in Daniel 8 "pertains" to the last days, not everything "takes place" in the last days.**

The statements in Daniel 8, verses 17 and 19, that the vision "pertains" to the last days and describes "what shall be in the last end," do not mean that every event and personality in that vision is bound to be situated in the future. It simply means that the grand finale — the rise of the Antichrist, or "king of fierce countenance" — will occur in the last days, and that all the other events are connected to that moment in some meaningful way, such as by providing some insight, basis, framework, or set-up.

A similar idiom is used in Daniel 2. As you may recall, that's the narrative where Daniel tells King Nebuchadnezzar that his entire statue pertains to "what shall be in the latter days" (v. 2:28). Yet we know the statue's "head of gold" referred only to ancient Babylon (v. 2:37-38), not to some future kingdom. Daniel says, "Thou, O king [Nebuchadnezzar], art a king of kings... **Thou art this head of gold**." In other words, although Daniel says that Nebuchadnezzar's vision pertains to "what shall be in the latter days," we understand that only the "feet of iron and clay" are actually situated in the end times. The rest of the statue pertains to kingdoms of old.

And that is precisely how the phrases in Daniel 8 — "at the time of the end shall be the vision" (v. 17) and "I will make thee know what shall be in the last end of the indignation"

(v. 19) — should be understood. The events and kingdoms of verses 8:20-22 are preliminary activities that belong to the days of Daniel, King Nebuchadnezzar, Darius the Mede, and Alexander the Great. The events of verses 8:23-26, however — including the rise of the "king of fierce countenance" — belong exclusively to the future, when the Antichrist comes to power.

c. **The phrase "in the latter part of their reign" actually means "at the end of the Gentile era."**

Finally, the phrase, "In the latter part of their reign," in Daniel 8:23, does not imply that all four kingdoms (the "four notable ones") will be reigning together in the last days, as many IAT expositors suggest. Instead, it simply means that the Little Horn will rise at the end of the **Gentile era**, a period of time that spans almost 2600 years.

A simple thought experiment will demonstrate that this is the proper way to read the phrase. Imagine, for example, participating in a discussion about ancient Rome and its 80-odd Caesars, when someone says, "The Battle of Narbonne occurred in the latter part of their reign." We don't imagine our friend is saying that all eighty Caesars were simultaneously reigning over the empire in 436 A.D. when the Battle of Narbonne took place. Instead, we immediately understand that our friend is talking about a brief moment in time, towards the end of the five-century *Roman era,* when that particular conflict was triggered and fought.

Likewise, the phrase "their reign" in Daniel 8:23 alludes to a 2600-year era characterized by the supremacy of Gentile empires, as opposed to the supremacy of Jesus and Israel. And thus, the "latter part of their reign" refers exclusively to the seven-year tribulation.

Consequently, verse 23 might be easier to understand if we simply substitute one phrase for the other:

> **Daniel 8:23** (NIV) – In the latter part of [**the 2600-year reign of the Gentiles**], when rebels have become completely wicked, a fierce-looking king, a master of intrigue, will arise.

This rendering shows that neither the Medo-Persian empire, nor the Greek empire, nor the empires of the Four Horns are required to exist (or return) in the last days, only that a Gentile kingdom — one which completes the era of Gentile rule — emerges at the end of the age, under the command of the Antichrist, to face Lord Jesus at the Battle of Armageddon. The following diagram might help make this more clear:

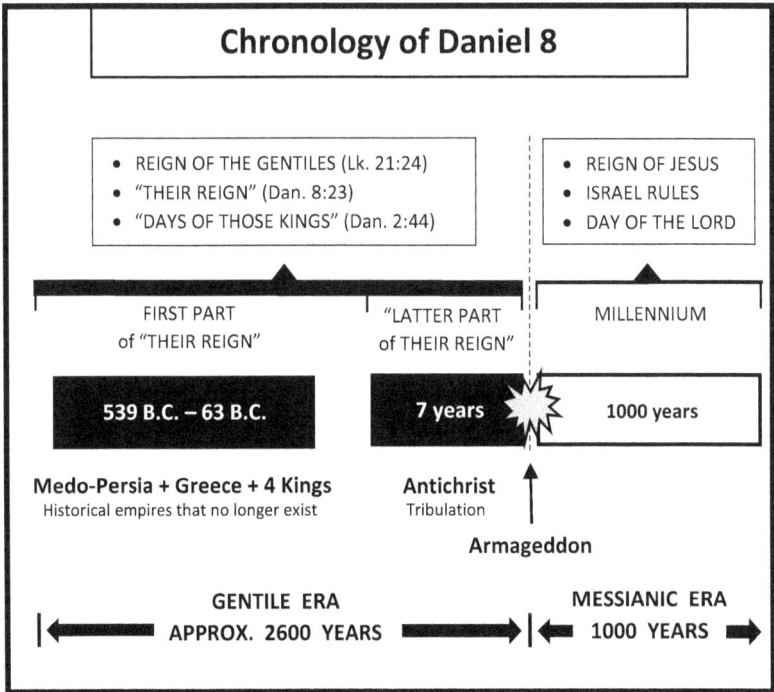

Chronology of Daniel 8

- REIGN OF THE GENTILES (Lk. 21:24)
- "THEIR REIGN" (Dan. 8:23)
- "DAYS OF THOSE KINGS" (Dan. 2:44)

- REIGN OF JESUS
- ISRAEL RULES
- DAY OF THE LORD

FIRST PART
of "THEIR REIGN"

"LATTER PART
of THEIR REIGN"

MILLENNIUM

539 B.C. – 63 B.C.

7 years

1000 years

Medo-Persia + Greece + 4 Kings
Historical empires that no longer exist

Antichrist
Tribulation

Armageddon

GENTILE ERA
APPROX. 2600 YEARS

MESSIANIC ERA
1000 YEARS

Chapter 4

SUMMARY and CONCLUSION

The previous chapter covered a lot of material. But the upshot is this: The Bible does not teach that the Antichrist will be a Muslim. Despite all the Islamic wars that have been launched against Israel, the unending terrorist attacks, and the apparent failure of a Roman Antichrist to materialize in Europe, the Bible clearly teaches that the Beast of the Apocalypse will be a Roman Caesar.

Consequently, all the arguments which underlie the Islamic Antichrist Theory disintegrate, once those claims are properly evaluated.

To review:

1. The "people" who were legally and practically responsible for destroying the Temple in 70 A.D. were not the local conscripts hired by Rome. They were the Romans themselves. Consequently, the Antichrist — who is the "prince" of those "people" — must be a Roman (Italian), not an Arab.

2. When Jesus described Pergamum as a place where "Satan's throne is" (Rev. 2:13), he was not implying that the enemy's seat of government was (or will be) physically located in that city. He was simply saying that Pergamum was filled with so much depravity and sin that Satan was "enthroned" in that area. The devil "ruled" the city. The phrase is meant as a metaphor for a concentration of paganism and perversion, not as a dot on a political map of the Middle East.

3. It's true that the title, "king of the north," is often connected with Middle East tyrants. However, it is not restricted to them. Instead, it applies to any commander who is likely to invade Israel via the northern gateway. Consequently, the title *could* refer to a European Antichrist, because European forces would normally enter the Holy Land via that route.

4. While it's true that both the Antichrist and the Arabs will attack Israel during the Tribulation — and that both the Antichrist and the Arabs will be defeated and punished by Christ upon his return — one cannot automatically conclude that the Antichrist is an Arab, based merely on those parallels. To draw that conclusion would be to rely on a fallacy known as a *false equivalence*.

   Indeed, when the Antichrist's homeland is specifically addressed in Scripture, the Bible clearly places it to the northwest of Israel (the Antichrist travels "south and east" to reach the "pleasant land.") This eliminates any possibility the Antichrist will come from Arabia, Persia, North Africa, or even Turkey, because none of those nations are located northwest of the Jews. Instead, all of those nations are situated either north, east, south, or southwest. Rome, on the other hand, *is* located northwest of the Holy Land.

5. The elements of the Beast's body in Revelation 13 — a lion's mouth, a bear's feet, and a leopard's core — do not reveal the Antichrist's religion, ethnicity, or national origin. Instead, they tell us the same things about the Antichrist as they did about the kings of Daniel 7: The Antichrist will be as "bold and proud" as a lion (like Nebuchadnezzar), as "strong" as a bear (like the forces of Cyrus of Persia), and as "fast and cunning" as a leopard (like Alexander the Great.) If this were not true — if these symbols pertained instead to the Antichrist's ethnicity or religion — then we'd be forced to conclude that the Antichrist is either a "Greek-Turk-Persian-Arab" (by race) or a "Greek Orthodox-Muslim" (by religion), contrivances which are virtually meaningless.

6. The Little Horn of Daniel 8 is an end-times figure, not a historical one. Therefore, Antiochus Epiphanes cannot be the Little Horn

of Daniel 8, and that means the borders of Antiochus' kingdom cannot be used to predict the territory from which the Antichrist will rise.

7. Inasmuch as Islam denies the deity of Jesus, it certainly meets the Bible's definition of an "anti-christ" religion (1 John 2:22). But that criterion is too broad to be useful. Other religions, such as Hinduism, Mormonism, Atheism, and Buddhism, also deny the deity of Christ. Resorting to 1 John therefore adds little weight to the Islamic Antichrist Theory.

8. The notion that Saudi Arabia or Mecca is the Whore of Babylon is patently false: both locales fail to match almost every detail provided in Scripture about the Whore. The Antichrist therefore cannot be tied to Islam through the symbols of Revelation 17.

9. While a superficial analysis of Daniel 2 and 7 suggests that the Fourth Empire might have been the Islamic Caliphate (because the caliphate was known for thoroughly "stamping the residue" of its enemies), a deeper analysis shows that the Roman Empire — as the one that actually killed the Messiah, "shattered" Jerusalem and the Temple, and then "stamped the residue" by killing or exiling the entire population of Judaea — is the one that's in view. The Antichrist will therefore come out of Rome, not out of the Islamic Caliphate.

10. The simultaneous destruction of all four sections of King Nebuchadnezzar's statue in Daniel 2 does not mean that the first three sections — Babylon, Medo-Persia, and Greece — will form the Antichrist's power-base. Instead, it simply means that *every* government of man will be destroyed by Christ when he returns, *and* that special punishment will be meted out to the descendants of Babylon, Medo-Persia, and Greece, as just payment for what their ancestors did — and for what they themselves have done — to the Jews.

11. Islamic eschatology does not come from the Holy Spirit, but from Muslim clerics who plagiarized certain prophecies in the Bible. It therefore cannot be used to determine the Antichrist's origin, or anything else about the Beast or the Tribulation.

12. Although a number of scriptures seem to refer to the Antichrist as "the Assyrian," the "king of Babylon," the "prince of Tyre," and the "king of the north," the very incongruity of these titles prevent using them as clues to the Antichrist's nationality. (Is the Antichrist Assyrian, Egyptian, Babylonian, Lydian, Tyrian, Russian, Persian, or something else?) Instead, these titles, to the extent they may apply to the Antichrist, are simply historical types, indicating that the Man of Sin — like Shalmaneser of Assyria and Nebuchadnezzar of Babylon — will be absolutely vicious and slaughter the Jews without mercy.

13. No Muslim would ever claim to be God or demand to be worshipped as such. Yet 2 Thessalonians 2:4 says the Antichrist will "exalteth himself above all that is called God, or that is worshipped; so that he as God sitteth in the temple of God, shewing himself that he is God." The Man of Sin therefore cannot be a Muslim.

14. Despite what many expositors believe about Ezekiel 38, the Antichrist (i.e., "Gog") is not the commander of Turkey, Egypt, Syria, Saudi Arabia, or any other Islamic nation listed in that chapter. Instead, he is their provocateur and mortal enemy. He will goad these countries into an all-out confrontation, thus pulling and "leading" them to Armageddon and hell, the way a prison guard "leads" convicted criminals to their doom. He is therefore not a Muslim caliph. He is a Roman Caesar whom God will use to draw the Arabs — and the rest of the planet — to Israel, so they can be executed and sent to their eternal prison at once.

15. The notion that the Goat of Daniel 8 symbolizes the leader of modern Turkey, and that an Islamic Antichrist will soon rise from the ashes of a war between Turkey and Iran is untenable. The

chronological break in this chapter places the Goat, the Ram, and the Four Notable Ones in the historical era, long past, while the Antichrist, or "little horn," is firmly set in an era still future to our own day.

Moreover, the details of the Goat and the Four Notable Ones perfectly match the story of Alexander the Great and the four generals who succeeded him, proving that the first part of Daniel 8 pertains to ancient history, not to some future Islamic Caliphate.

In light of all the preceding evidence, only one conclusion is possible: The Antichrist cannot be a Muslim. Nor can his empire consist of the territory or people that comprised Assyria, Babylon, Persia, the Islamic Caliphates, or even the Ottoman Empire. Indeed, there is no scriptural basis *whatsoever* for thinking that the Antichrist will be a Muslim. One simply cannot derive an "Islamic Antichrist" from the pages of the Judeo-Christian Bible.

Instead, the evidence consistently obtained from the Word of God is that the Antichrist will be a Roman. He will come out of Europe. And he will rule a revived Roman Empire drawn from the religious, cultural, geographic, genetic, linguistic, legal, and architectural remnants of Caesar's empire, that is, the European Union. (Please see the following chapter.)

Chapter 5

THE ANTICHRIST WILL BE A ROMAN

SINCE WE NOW KNOW the Antichrist cannot be a Muslim, the question is: What will he be? In my opinion, the overwhelming evidence points to only one possibility — the Antichrist will be a Roman.

The following three arguments represent just a few of the many lines of reasoning that prove the Beast will come from Rome. The rest are covered in my books, *The Antichrist* and *Empire of the Antichrist*.

DIVINE RETRIBUTION

The principle of divine retribution is well-established in Scripture. It states that the elements of a crime must be replicated in the punishment. Eye for eye, tooth for tooth, life for life. Divine retribution is God's way of insuring that the penalty for each sin is just and equitable.

One can see this principle at work in many well-known Bible stories. For example, Jacob hid his identity from his father in order to steal his brother's birthright, but then Jacob's father-in-law hid his daughter's identity in order to "steal" another seven years of work from Jacob. Another time, King Sennacherib of Assyria threatened to slaughter every citizen within the walls of Jerusalem, but then, on the very eve of that event, an Angel of the Lord slaughtered every soldier in the Assyrian camp (185,000 men). Still again, Pharaoh once drowned all the firstborn of Israel to prevent the rise of a deliverer, but then God delivered the Hebrews by drowning Pharaoh and killing all the firstborn of Egypt. Many more examples could be cited.

Hence, if we apply the principle of divine retribution to the Antichrist, and *focus* that principle on the ethnic group he is likely to come from, then only one conclusion is possible: Since Jesus was executed under the authority of an **Italian Caesar** (Tiberius), then it must be an **Italian Caesar** (the Antichrist) whom Jesus will return to execute.

THE EIGHTH KING

According to Revelation 17, the Antichrist, or "beast," is the last in a line of eight notable kings:

> **Revelation 17:9-11** (NKJV) – Here is the mind which has wisdom. The seven heads are seven mountains on which the woman sits, and **they are seven kings**; five have fallen, one is, the other has not yet come; and when he comes, he must remain a little while. **The beast which was and is not, is himself also an eighth and is *one* of the seven**, and he goes to destruction.

Here's what to note about these verses: When these Seven Kings first appear a few chapters earlier (Rev. 12:3), they are said to be wearing their crowns. That may seem like an innocuous detail, but it's actually the key to determining their nationality. Why? Because the *wearing of crowns* tells us these kings were *in power* during the events that follow in the subsequent narrative (i.e., the storyline of chapter 12.)

Those events were: the birth of Jesus (v. 12:5), the attempt by Satan to assassinate him (v. 12:4), the ascension of Christ to the throne of the Father (v. 12:5), Satan's eviction from heaven immediately thereafter (v. 12:9), the flight of Jewish believers to the city of Pella in 67 A.D. for a sojourn of 3½ years (v. 12:6), and the dispersal of the Jews throughout the earth, beginning in 70 A.D. (v. 12:13-16).

All of these events occurred during the Roman era. And that means the "seven kings" through whom the Dragon was operating must have been **seven emperors who were in power during the old Roman**

Empire. In fact, they were Augustus, Tiberius, Caligula, Claudius, Nero, Domitian, and Romulus Augustus. And all seven were *Italian*.[61]

Consequently, since the Antichrist will *cap this line* of Caesars as the "eighth king," and since he is actually said to be *one of the seven*, the Antichrist must be an **Italian**, as well.

DANIEL'S 70TH WEEK

According to the book of Daniel, God allotted exactly seventy weeks of years to the Jewish people — that is, 490 years, beginning in 445 B.C. — to complete his dealings with their sin and rebellion.

Significantly, all seventy weeks were pre-ordained to occur under the dispensation of Law. In other words, throughout that entire timeline of 490 years, the religious and civil code of Moses would be observed by the Jews, there would be a Temple and a Sanhedrin, the Gentiles would not be directly involved in the plan of Redemption (i.e., the Church would not be present), a Jewish high priest would serve as both religious and civil leader of Israel (there would be no Davidic king sitting on Israel's throne), and the nation would suffer at the hands of foreign despots.

Those were the conditions that existed when Jesus first offered the kingdom to Israel in 32 A.D., the year which marked the end of the 69th Week. The Temple stood in Jerusalem, the Sanhedrin sat as a parliament, the Jews observed the Law of Moses, the Church did not exist, a high priest (who compromised with Rome) served as national leader, and a ruthless **Italian Caesar** held the Jewish people in the grip of his iron fist. That's how it was in Israel in 33 A.D. when Jesus was rejected and "cut off" — or put to death (Dan. 9:26) — thus leaving one week, the 70th, still to play out.

---

[61] Please see *Empire of the Antichrist* (Positron Books, 2020) to learn why these particular Caesars are in view. Also note: The first six Caesars were Italian on both their fathers' and mothers' sides. However, to be fair, the seventh, Romulus Augustus, was Italian on his father's side only (his mother was German.)

Consequently, when that 70th Week begins and the countdown resumes (immediately following the Rapture), the conditions that existed in 33 A.D. must be reconstituted. The conditions under which Jesus *first* offered to save the Jews must exist when Jesus offers to save them *again*. Otherwise, Jesus would not be offering the Jews of today the same contract he offered their forefathers, a scenario which is absolutely unthinkable.

The verses below confirm that Jesus will offer to save today's Jews under the same conditions that he offered to save their ancestors:

> **Matthew 23:39** (NKJV) – For **I** [Jesus] say unto **you** [i.e., you Jews who live under the dispensation of Law and the oppression of Rome], **you** shall see me no more till **you** say, "Blessed is he who comes in the name of the Lord."

> **1 Samuel 15:29** (HCSB) – Furthermore, the Eternal One of Israel does not lie or change His mind, for **He is not man who changes his mind**.

> **Numbers 23:19** (NASB) – God is not a man, that he should lie, Nor a son of man, that He should repent; Has He said, and will He not do it? **Or has He spoken, and will He not make it good**?

Consequently, when Jesus returns at the end of the 70th Week, the Jews must be living as a sovereign nation in their ancestral homeland, the Temple must be standing in Jerusalem, there must be a Sanhedrin, the Church cannot be present on the earth, a duplicitous prime minister must be in power in Israel, and a ruthless **Italian Caesar** must be holding the Jews in a devastating iron grip. That is the only way the terms of Jesus' original offer to save the Jews from the fury of Rome (Mt. 3:2 and 23:37-38) can genuinely be assessed to be "identical."

And that means the Antichrist — the final king of the Gentiles — has to be an **Italian**, just as the king of Rome was in 33 A.D.

SUMMARY

These three concepts, in addition to many others, prove beyond a shadow of a doubt that the Antichrist will be an Italian. He will soon rise to international prominence, confirm the Treaty of Daniel 9:27, and then take charge of a ten-nation military force in Europe, which he will use to drag North Africa and the Middle East into a series of deadly wars. At the end of his seven-year reign he will then use those forces to fight against Christ at the Battle of Armageddon, but he will be captured and thrown alive into the Lake of Fire.[62]

---

[62] For more information on the Antichrist's nationality and power-base, please see my books, *The Antichrist* and *Empire of the Antichrist*.

Chapter 6

KNOWLEDGE AND TRAVEL
SHALL VASTLY INCREASE

SO FAR, we've learned that the Antichrist *cannot be* a Muslim. Instead, he must be an Italian, and he will soon come out of a revived Roman Empire. But *how soon?* Could it be as soon as next year? Or perhaps within the next five years? And if it is that soon, then what are the signs that prove it?

The fact is, there are dozens of signs which prove that our generation stands at the brink of the Apocalypse. These include such things as:

- The advent of nuclear warheads and other weapons of mass destruction that can eradicate the entire population of earth (Zech. 14:12; Mt. 24:22).

- The rise of a powerful movement, based in Rome, to unite all religions (Rev. 17:2, 15, 18).

- The creation of a fledgling world government in the form of the United Nations (Rev. 13:7).

- The return of the Roman Empire in 1948 in the form of the 10-nation Western European Union, now called the European Intervention Initiative or EI2 (Dan. 7:24; Rev. 17:12).

But there's another sign which proves our world is on the verge of the Tribulation, and it's one of the most convincing of all. It is the explosion in travel and knowledge that began at the turn of the last century, a phenomenon that Daniel predicted over 2500 years ago!

Consider the following. In 1900 human society was little more than a collection of far-flung enclaves, barely held together by telegraph wires, wind-blown ships, and horses-drawn carriages. Today, we are a "global village" dominated by endless highways, bullet trains, jet aircraft, satellites, television, radio, the internet, cell phones, super-computers, and drones. Everyone is now connected to everyone else, at the touch of a button.

In 1899, Charles H. Duell, Commissioner of the U.S. Patent Office, famously said, "Everything that can be invented has been invented." He was spectacularly wrong. At that time, human knowledge was doubling every century. But today, our knowledge is doubling every 13 months, and some believe it will soon double every 12 hours, once the internet is fully built-out.

The prophet Daniel predicted this acceleration in technology over twenty-five hundred years ago:

> **Daniel 12:4** (KJV) — But thou, O Daniel, shut up the words, and seal the book, even to the **time of the end**: **many shall run to and fro**, and **knowledge shall be increased**.

> **Daniel 12: 4** (TLB) — But Daniel, keep this prophecy a secret; seal it up so that it will not be understood until the **end times**, when **travel** and **education** [knowledge] **shall be vastly increased!**

Notice that the increase in "travel" and "knowledge" is directly tied to the "time of the end." This means that the astounding explosion in science, technology, and transportation which has dominated our planet since World War II *could not have happened* until the final generation arrived. Yet we have seen this phenomenon take place with our own eyes. And that means you and I are living on borrowed time.

Consider this fact: The current population of earth is the very first generation to witness such unparalleled technologies as:

- Artificial intelligence that can out-think any human

- Lasers, computers, and video recording devices

- Aerial drones fitted with guns, cameras, missiles, and GPS

- Mechanical exo-skeletons that can turn human troops into "terminators"

- Robotic horses, snakes, sharks, dogs, insects, and other "animals," specially created for police and military operations

- Weapons of mass destruction, including such devices as nuclear bombs, chemical agents, and biological pathogens—the very things needed to make "stars fall," "the sky roll up," "sores break out," and "one-third of the earth's vegetation burn up."

- Satellite television and the internet, which for the first time in history make possible the instantaneous, worldwide viewing of the Two Witnesses' bodies lying dead in the streets of Jerusalem (Rev. 11:9), along with the Antichrist's sacrilegious antics in the Holy of Holies (Mt. 24:15-16).

- RFID chips, biometric scanners, and recombinant DNA, the very elements that will likely make up the Mark of the Beast and doom millions of people to hell.

But there's more…

THE PROPHETIC KNOWLEDGE EXPLOSION

In addition to the unparalleled advances in mankind's technology (much of which will be used in fulfillment of the events prophesied to take place during the Apocalypse), a significant number of theologians also believe the same scriptures point to a stunning increase in our understanding of **Bible prophecy** towards the end of the age.

According to this view, as the Tribulation approaches, there will be a sudden and dramatic rise in the Church's ability to solve certain passages and connect all the dots of Daniel and the Apocalypse. By the grace of God, students of prophecy will finally be able to unlock and correlate the characters and sayings that have long resisted the Church's best efforts.

I agree with that assessment, and here's why: At least four Old Testament prophets, including Daniel, said this is precisely what would happen as the "time of testing" approached:

- **Jeremiah 23:20** — **The anger of the LORD** will not turn back Until He has executed and performed the thoughts of His heart. **In the latter days you will understand it perfectly.**

- **Joel 2:28** — And it shall come to pass **afterward**, that I will pour out my spirit upon all flesh; and **your sons and your daughters shall prophesy, your old men shall dream dreams, your young men shall see visions.**

- **Amos 3:7** — Surely the Lord GOD does nothing, **Unless He reveals His secret to His servants the prophets.**

- **Daniel 12:9-10** — And he said, Go thy way, Daniel: for the words are closed up and sealed till **the time of the end**. Many shall be purified, and made white, and tried; but the wicked shall do wickedly: and none of the wicked shall understand; but **the wise shall understand.**

In fulfillment of these predictions, the Church's prophetic IQ has risen by a greater degree over the last seven decades than at any other time since the days of the apostles. As of 2019, the modern Church knows more about the major players and events of the Apocalypse than any previous generation of believers.

For instance, we now know (with a very high degree of confidence) that:

- The Fourth Empire of Daniel is the empire of Rome.

- The Whore of Babylon is the city of Rome.

- The Antichrist will be a Roman (Italian) peace negotiator.

- The Seven Heads of the Beast stand for the Roman emperors Augustus, Tiberius, Caligula, Claudius, Nero, Domitian, and Romulus Augustus.

- The Ten Horns of the Beast are ten "kings" from the revived Roman Empire (the European Intervention Initiative), and probably include the heads of state of France, Belgium, Luxembourg, The Netherlands, Spain, Portugal Greece, Britain, Germany, and Italy.[63]

- "Gog" is another name for the Antichrist (in Ezekiel 38), and his "war" is Armageddon.

- The final countdown began in 1948, when Israel returned as a nation, and the Roman Empire returned in the form of the Western European Union (now the "EI2".)

- The Vatican is the religious aspect of "Babylon." It is also the center of ecumenism, and will assist the False Prophet in leading the masses to embrace the Antichrist.

- Man's depravity and transgressions have finally "come to the full." [64]

---

[63] These particular countries were the ten full-fledged members of the original Western European Union (WEU). In 2018 the WEU was resurrected in the form of the European Intervention Initiative (EI2), a military alliance that will (in my opinion) carry out the Antichrist's Armageddon campaign, in accordance with Revelation 17:13-14. Please see my book, *Empire of the Antichrist* (2020).

[64] For the first time in history, our world is utterly consumed by the most abominable sins ever conceived in the heart of man. These include such outrageous crimes as sex trafficking, terrorist massacres, pedophilia, and full-term abortion.

A BRIEF HISTORY OF TIME

Up until the 20th Century, the prophecies of Revelation and Daniel were the province of theologians and seminary students. Few members of the general public were interested in what the Bible had to say about Armageddon and the judgements of the Tribulation. Most people realized that neither the technology nor the political arrangements required to fulfill the prophecies of the Apocalypse were in place. Significantly, the Jews had not yet been re-established in their ancient homeland, and devices capable of wiping mankind off the face of the earth had not yet been invented.

Then came 1948 and the rebirth of Israel, along with the advent of nuclear weapons, ICBMs (Inter-Continental Ballistic Missiles), computers, television, and supersonic jets. And with these, the public's interest in Bible prophecy began to skyrocket. Both theologian and layman understood the meaning of the re-establishment of Israel and the advent of unprecedented technologies: It meant that the Apocalypse was now inevitable. It meant that our planet was finally set on a course that would inexorably lead to Armageddon.

As a result, a number of preachers began teaching that time was running out for our world. People across America tuned in to these sermons with rapt attention and tried their best to grasp all the details. But the complexities were often hard to digest.

In an attempt to fill in the missing pieces, many Christians turned to their local libraries and searched for detailed explanations of Daniel and Revelation. But the number of readily accessible books on Bible prophecy was decidedly meager. Most of the titles were long and difficult treatises. Others were introductory pamphlets, too thin on details to satisfy people's thirst for knowledge.

All of that changed in 1970, however, when a previously unknown writer by the name of Hal Lindsey published his ground-breaking work, *The Late, Great Planet Earth*. Lindsey's genius was not that he had discovered some new "revelation from God" about the end times, but that he was able to make the most difficult passages and concepts in Revelation easy to understand. He did this by using a conversational tone, coupled with clear and thorough analysis, which enabled people to both grasp and discuss the Apocalypse with greater ease than ever before. From that point forward, the number of popular books on Bible prophecy skyrocketed.

Today, a significant cross-section of Christians are literally devouring every available piece of information regarding the end times, and talented authors (anointed by God) are bringing many new and exciting observations to the forefront. They are providing us with answers and insight no one ever thought possible.

This expansion of end-time knowledge is also reflected in the number of ministries, seminars, and conferences that focus on Bible prophecy. Indeed, attendance at these venues has soared to all-time highs. This year alone, in 2019, there have been more than two dozen major summits in America on Bible prophecy, and in almost every case the event has drawn hundreds (if not thousands) of Christians from across the country. That level of interest, and the amount of new information and insight that it takes to support such a phenomenon, shows that God is in the midst of delivering on his promise to reveal the details and meaning of Daniel and the Apocalypse, as the final countdown draws to a close.

CONCLUSION

The unprecedented increase in travel and human knowledge over the last seventy years, plus the increasing ability of the Church, through the grace of God, to unlock dozens of previously unyielding prophetic mysteries, tells us we're at the end of the age. Truly, if we're not standing at the threshold of the Tribulation, then prophecy has no meaning.

But prophecy does have meaning! And the fulfillment of Daniel 12:4 — the sudden and overwhelming increase in mankind's scientific knowledge, along with the Church's new-found ability to comprehend the prophetic Word — proves that we stand at the threshold of Christ's return.

The Angel was clear when he said that those who are wise will see these things and recognize what they portend:

> **Daniel 12:9-10** — And he said, Go thy way, Daniel: for the words are closed up and sealed till the **time of the end**... [N]one of the wicked shall understand; but **the wise shall understand.**

Let us therefore take the prophetic Word of God to heart, and in anticipation of Christ's soon return for the Church, put our house in order. Then, having rededicated ourselves to the Lord, let us take the Good News of Christ's amazing gift to a lost and dying world, while there is still time to do so. In that way, we will show ourselves "wise," and be counted "worthy to escape all these things that shall come to pass, and to stand before the Son of man" (Lk. 21:36).

Chapter 7

THE ONLY WAY TO THE FATHER

ACCORDING TO A NUMBER of recent surveys, many Christians now believe there are other ways to the Father aside from the biblical path of simple repentance and an abiding faith in Christ. As incredible as it may seem, some 70% of Evangelicals now say that other traditions — religions based on good deeds and ancient rituals — have the power to save a person on the Day of Judgment.

Catholicism is a case in point. No one can deny that Catholics are some of the most stalwart members of society. They have a deep love of family, and they're dedicated to protecting unborn life. The charities they run are world-renowned for helping the poor and protecting the outcast. Some of the greatest leaders in society are Catholics, and the contributions of Catholics to the making of America are legendary. We owe them our deepest love and respect.

However, many Evangelicals now believe that Catholics are saved *simply because* they acknowledge the virgin birth, the deity of Jesus, and the blood atonement of the Cross. Those who subscribe to this notion seem to forget that Catholic doctrine then adds to these fundamentals by mandating a host of "good works," thereby denying the power of the Cross *alone* to make us fully acceptable to God. In the Vatican's opinion, one isn't saved by merely repenting and trusting in Jesus. Instead, one must also join the Church of Rome and participate in several forms of "good works." These include such things as confession, penance, communion, attending mass, going though purgatory, praying to "saints," obeying the pope, and petitioning "Mary" for the forgiveness of sins.

Not to be outdone, another school of thought teaches that practicing Jews are in good standing with God, because Jesus did not present himself to them as their Messiah. Therefore, the argument goes, the Jews are still under the Old Testament system of good deeds, rituals, and ethical behavior. As long as they follow these customs sincerely, they will be saved on the Day of Judgment.

Let me start by saying that the Jewish people are the only reason any of us will be saved on the Day of Judgment. It is thanks to the Jews and their willingness to endure untold suffering (for centuries) that we have the Bible, the prophets, and the Savior. As Jesus once said, salvation is of the Jews (John 4:22). Their contributions to the betterment of mankind are almost without limit and the debt we owe them can never be fully repaid. We must love and respect them, and always remember they are God's special people.

Yet, at the same time, we cannot ignore the scriptures which clearly state that Jesus did, in fact, present himself as their Messiah (Mt. 26:63-64; Lk. 4:17-29), and that his death and resurrection renders the old Mosaic system powerless to save anyone (Mt. 5:20; Rom. 3:20; Gal. 2:16, 21). Hence, no man can be saved by his own righteousness, ethics, or adherence to ceremony.

The tragedy about all of this isn't that so many Evangelicals have suddenly forgotten the Gospel, it's that we've simply lost our nerve to proclaim it. We are afraid of offending Catholics and Jews, and so we've compromised the Good News and have missed the very opportunity and platform that God has given us to reach these precious people.

I realize there's always a bit of trepidation whenever one witnesses to a person of another faith. Many non-Christians instinctively recoil from anyone who attempts to bring them the Gospel because, in the past, they have suffered at the hands of those who call themselves Christians. We Christians therefore tend to avoid bringing up the subject when amongst our Catholic and Jewish neighbors. It's too disruptive, we don't want to be rejected, and we feel a little bit guilty for what other so-called "Christians" have done to these people. I fully understand the situation.

However, to allow tens of millions of people to continue believing they're on the road to heaven, when they're actually on the boulevard to hell, is not love. It is a dereliction of duty. And it will result in consequences far worse than anything Catholics and Jews have had to endure so far.

Let me ask the reader: Can anyone call on the name of Mary and expect to be saved from the Judgment? Can the repetition of memorized prayers or the performance of a dozen acts of penance add to the blood atonement of Christ? Can anyone point to their heritage, race, or ethnic group and claim, thereby, to be guiltless before God? Does the rite of circumcision, or a young man's bar mitzvah, wash away the stain of sin? Is God pleased when a person consistently prays to dead "saints" and statues, or when he consistently denies that Jesus's blood is the only acceptable payment for the forgiveness of sins?

The Bible answered these questions two thousand years ago:

> **John 14:6** – I am the way, the truth, and the life: no man cometh unto the Father, but by me.

> **Acts 4:12** – Neither is there salvation in any other: for there is none other name under heaven given among men, whereby we must be saved.

> **Matthew 3:9** – And think not to say within yourselves, We have Abraham to our father: for I say unto you, that God is able of these stones to raise up children unto Abraham.

> **Exodus 20:4-6** – Thou shalt not make unto thee any graven image, or any likeness *of any thing* that *is* in heaven above, or that *is* in the earth beneath, or that *is* in the water under the earth: Thou shalt not bow down thyself to them, nor serve them: for I the LORD thy God *am* a jealous God, visiting the iniquity of the fathers upon

the children unto the third and fourth *generation* of them that hate me; And shewing mercy unto thousands of them that love me, and keep my commandments.

In plain language, it is impossible to be saved from the Judgment, apart from true repentance and an abiding faith in Jesus Christ alone. When the books in heaven are opened and a person's sins are exposed, he (or she) cannot call on the name of a pope, a saint, or even Moses or Mary, and expect to be saved from God's wrath. We cannot expect our "good deeds," or the fact that we're a part of God's "chosen people," to pay for our transgressions. God has already stated that, in regards to establishing our guilt or innocence at the Great White Throne Judgment, our "ethical behavior" and "good deeds" will be counted as *filthy rags* (Is. 64:6).

To repeat: Not even a person's Catholic credentials or Jewish bloodline will save him. As Peter once said regarding the ability of a person to be saved by his ethnicity or religion: "Of a truth I perceive that God is no respecter of persons" (Acts 10:34).

The reality is that the only way to avoid the penalty for breaking God's Law — that is, for lying, stealing, cheating, coveting what belongs to other people, dishonoring our parents, and dishonoring God — is to turn from sin *now* and to follow Jesus. And, if we truly love our Jewish and Catholic friends, co-workers, and family members, we will bring them that message, even if it means risking their displeasure.

What does it mean to follow Jesus? It means to decide that we want to stop sinning (a person repents). And it must be followed by a decision to live for the Lord (a person exhibits faith). How do we live for the Lord? By simply following the new desires that God puts in our hearts, the moment we surrender to him (Ez. 36:26; Phil. 2:13). We read the Bible and do what it says, yet always trusting in nothing but Jesus' work on the Cross to save us. We then watch the Holy Spirit produce "good fruit" in our lives, the fruit of "love, joy, peace, forbearance, kindness, goodness, faithfulness, gentleness and self-control" (Gal. 5:22-23; NIV). We also look for the fruit of saved souls, as we witness to people and spread the Good News (John 4:35). We see a sharp decrease in the amount of sin in our personal lives, and a notable increase in the level of purity — *not* out of our own effort, but because the Holy Spirit is transforming us and creating a new nature within us, one that *naturally wants* to abandon sin and embrace righteousness.

My prayer is that all good Christians will return to the Gospel and start preaching it without regard to a person's religious background or ethnicity. We cannot create "carve outs" for certain religions, or make excuses for not witnessing to Catholics and Jews. *All* men need to hear the Good News of Christ's salvation. And that includes all Catholics, Jews, Muslims, Mormons, Buddhists, Hindus, Wiccans, Atheists, pagans, members of the Watchtower Society, and even quite a few Evangelicals. We must never forget that sometimes we're the only person who will present the Gospel to these precious souls before they step into eternity.

God grant us the strength to preach the Word, both in season and out of season, and to preach it without fear or favor. The stakes are infinite…and irrevocable.

AFTERWORD

ALLOW ME to express my deepest gratitude to the Lord for my salvation and for his multiplied blessings. His guidance and support throughout this project have been utterly amazing—and quite humbling.

I would also like to thank the innumerable pastors, scholars, and authors who have laid the groundwork for me, by providing laymen (such as myself) with access to their research and conclusions through such media as books, videos, and live sermons. Your works are precious.

To the reader, thank you for taking the time to consider this short collection of thoughts. I hope it will bless you in some way and help you draw closer to Christ.

Please understand, this book assumes the reader has a good handle on the basics of Bible prophecy. *The Islamic Antichrist Myth* is not meant to provide a broad overview of the end times. It is meant to disprove a particular theory of eschatology, namely, the mistaken belief that the Antichrist will be a Muslim. Nevertheless, I have tried to guide the reader (where appropriate) by clarifying how the concepts presented in this work fit within the overall prophetic tapestry.

With these thoughts in mind, permit me to briefly state my approach to the chronology of Bible prophecy:

- Futurist – The vast majority of the events of Revelation 4-22 are still future. They were not fulfilled during the Jewish Rebellion in 70 A.D., nor are they a mere allegory of the struggle between good and evil.

- Pre-Tribulational – The Rapture will take place before the Tribulation begins. Christ will come for his Church and take her to heaven before the start of Daniel's 70th Week (before the treaty of Daniel 9:27 is signed.) Furthermore, the Rapture is "imminent," meaning it can happen at a moment. There are no prophetic signs which have to precede it.

- Pre-Millennial – Christ will return physically to the earth prior to the start of his one-thousand-year reign from Jerusalem.

- Dispensational – Throughout history, men have always been justified by turning from sin (repenting) and obeying God's commands (exhibiting faith). But God has divided history into seven epochs, or dispensations, specifying, in each, how people are to express their faith at that moment. These epochs include: Innocence, Conscience, Human Government, Promise, Law, Grace, and The Kingdom. Currently, we're in the dispensation of Grace.

Additionally, as we go through this study, we should always remember that the hero of prophecy is Jesus of Nazareth. He alone is the one who redeems mankind from eternal destruction. He is therefore the focus and fulfillment of God's prophetic Word, a fact which yields at least two very important axioms:

- **Prophecy is Christ-centered** – The Bible repeatedly declares that Jesus Christ is the center and fullness of prophecy. Consequently, the prophetic Word always pivots on one of two things: Jesus' First Advent and the Cross, or Jesus' Second Advent and Armageddon (and, by extension, the Millennial Kingdom.) Of all the concepts that guide our study of eschatology, this is by far the most important. Prophecy centers on Christ:

  > **John 5:39** (NKJV) – You search the Scriptures, for in them you think you have eternal life; and these are they which testify of Me.

  > **Acts 3:20-21** – And he shall send Jesus Christ…which God hath spoken by the mouth of all His holy prophets since the world began.

- **Prophecy takes place within the context of Israel** – Immediately beneath the first axiom is a corollary: The prophecies of Scripture always unfold within the context of Israel and the Jews. Without the Jews, there are no prophets, there is no Bible, and we have no Messiah. Indeed, it is because of the Jewish people's willingness to endure untold suffering and sorrow—for centuries—that we have a chance to escape the Judgment. As the apostle John once said, "[S]alvation is of the Jews" (Jn. 4:22). For these reasons, the land and people of Israel will always be at the center of Bible prophecy. They are God's special children, and neither the Church nor anyone else will replace them.

Accordingly, eschatology always focuses on, and unfolds within, the geography, culture, events, politics, chastisements, victories, miracles, and people of Israel:

> **Romans 9:3-5** – [M]y countrymen according to the flesh, who are Israelites, to whom *pertain* the adoption, the glory, the covenants, the giving of the law, the service *of God*, and the promises.

The impact of the above two axioms is this: Every major prophecy of Scripture is tethered to the person of Jesus Christ and his mission to save mankind, and especially his mission to save the nation of Israel. Therefore, any analysis which fails to include or acknowledge this crucial aspect of the prophetic Word is inherently flawed.

In closing this section, it might be helpful to review the "Rules of Interpretation," beginning on page 127. These are ten basic guidelines that will help keep us on track with the various prophecies and associated narratives. Whenever the discussion requires it, the appropriate rule will be cited so you can follow my reasoning (e.g., "Rule 2"). The section is pretty short and I think you'll find it both fascinating and informative.

P.S. – You'll notice I quote from a number of different Bible versions throughout this essay. Some might question this practice, but I wanted to make sure that, in every case, the intent of the original words was expressed as closely as possible. Unfortunately, in English, there is no version of Scripture which is always accurate. Some versions add words, others delete words, and some even change words. I therefore make it a point to use the version which, I believe, most closely reflects the original Hebrew and Greek, and which preserves the essential meaning of the verse I am quoting. My goal is to be accurate.

APPENDIX A

RULES OF INTERPRETATION

EVERY SERIOUS RESEARCHER knows that to correlate and make sense of volumes of data, one must first establish some basic assumptions and rules of interpretation. That's because our rules and assumptions provide the logical framework on which to hang our data and build reasonable theories and conclusions.

This is true regardless of whether one is engaged in archaeology, astrophysics, crime scene analysis, or Bible prophecy. Our rules of interpretation dictate whether we will solve the puzzle or keep running in circles.

I have therefore compiled a number of ground rules for this study and placed them below. I think most expositors will agree they're both useful and reasonable, because students of prophecy have been applying these guidelines for decades. The key is to apply them with discipline. If we truly wish to unlock the treasures that God has hidden in prophecy, we must stick to these rules as closely as possible.

Accordingly, whenever the discussion calls for it, the appropriate rule will be cited so you can follow my reasoning. I think you'll find this section both fascinating and informative.

1. When the plain sense makes sense, seek no other sense.

    o   This axiom was coined by Dr. David L. Cooper of The Biblical Research Society in the early 1900s. The full hermeneutic reads: "**When the plain sense of Scripture makes common sense, seek no other sense**; therefore, take every word at its primary, ordinary, usual, literal meaning unless the facts of the immediate context, studied in the light of related passages and axiomatic and fundamental truths, indicate clearly otherwise."

o Allow me to translate the essence of this statement: When the narrative reads like a news report or an eyewitness account, then take it as a news report or an eyewitness account. When the text says "this is a parable," then take it as a parable and find out what each symbol stands for. (Usually, **the symbols will be explained right in the passage.** If not, they will be explained **somewhere else in Scripture.**)

When the narrative uses hyperbole, such as when a person says, "I'm so hungry I could eat a horse," or, "He's ten times smarter than me," then we know exaggerated language is being used to emphasize a point. We don't need to take the phrase literally. Likewise, when a prophet says he sees a sign or a vision—either on earth or in heaven—then we know that sign or vision stands for something real. Our job then is to determine what that "something" is from the **surrounding text,** or from a **relevant passage elsewhere in Scripture.**

2. There must be no *re*-interpretation of *the* interpretation.

o Once a symbol is explained in the text, that explanation cannot be re-interpreted by an expositor to mean something else. Otherwise, the authoritative definition (from God) is voided and we immediately depart into error. This may sound obvious enough, but many expositors ignore this critical guideline and then re-interpret the very definition provided in the passage. The resulting confusion has led to unrecoverable errors.

For example, even though the text of Revelation 17 explicitly says the Seven Heads in that passage represent seven kings, many expositors skirt that definition and then re-interpret the seven *kings* to mean seven *kingdoms*. This one error (by itself) is perhaps the single greatest impediment to solving the mysteries of the Apocalypse. **If an explicit definition is provided in the text, we must accept it "as is." Barring**

any additional statements within the interpretation itself, we must not change that interpretation or go beyond it:

> **Deuteronomy 4:2** – Ye shall not add unto the word which I command you, neither shall ye diminish ought from it, that ye may keep the commandments of the Lord your God which I command you.

[Also see Proverbs 30:5-6 and Revelation 22:18-19.]

3. Numbers carry both literal and symbolic meaning in prophecy.

    o   **The number 3** can literally refer to three items on a list (such as the Three Woes of Revelation 8.) But it can also indicate the **beginning, middle, and end of a set.** For example, Daniel's "seventy weeks" (in Daniel 9) certainly consist of seventy weeks (specifically, seventy weeks of years.) But the seventy are divided into three groups to indicate the beginning weeks (7), the middle weeks (62), and the final week (1). (Please see chart below.)

A CONSTRUCT OF 3 RELATED ITEMS INDICATES THE CHRONOLOGICAL BEGINNING, MIDDLE, AND END OF A SET

SET	BEGINNING	MIDDLE	END
Bible	Genesis ("Beginnings")	Exodus – Jude	Revelation (End of the Age)
Harvests of Israel[1]	First Fruits	Main Harvest	Gleanings
Restoration of Israel[2]	Bones	Flesh	Breath
The Book of Revelation[3]	Things already seen	Things that are	Things that shall be hereafter
70 Weeks of Daniel[4]	7 Weeks	62 Weeks	1 Week
Tribulation Judgements	Seals	Trumpets	Bowls
Caesars of Ancient Rome[5]	5 Fallen	1 Living	1 Coming

Notes: 1 - Ex. 23:16 and Lev. 19:9-10
2 - Ez. 37:7-10
3 - Rev. 1:19
4 - Dan. 9:24-27
5 - Rev. 17:10

o **The number 7** represents a complete group or an entire set. This is true even if that set has more than seven components. For example, the seven churches of Revelation are indeed seven literal churches. But they also stand for the complete set of churches that exist from the time of John to the Rapture. In other words, the seven churches of Revelation cover the entire church age. They effectively represent tens of thousands of congregations, over a 2000-year period.

Consequently, the number 7 expresses: **perfection or a complete set**.

4.   God builds precept upon precept.

o   God is not the author of confusion. Instead, he sets a pattern or an outline, and then adds all the details to that outline in a progressive manner. Line upon line, precept upon precept, until the entire picture has formed—**yet always in accordance with the original pattern** (Is. 28:10). Once the pattern or outline is set, all subsequent outlines and data must align with the original scheme. Why? Because there *must be* a fixed point of reference, a grand super-structure, in order to make sense of all the information. This is key.

Indeed, this principle is so fundamental to the interpretation of God's Word that it appears in the very first book of the Bible. Specifically, in Genesis 37:5-8 and 9-10, God told Joseph, through two separate dreams, that his family would bow down to him. The symbols in each dream were *different* (sheaves vs. stars), but the message in each case was *identical* (your family will honor your authority). Similarly, in Genesis 41:1-7 and 41:25, God told Pharaoh, through two separate dreams, that Egypt would experience seven years of plenty, followed by seven years of famine. The symbols in each dream were *different* (cows vs. corn stalks), but the message in each case was *identical* (store up your goods before the curse of God comes.)

Indeed, anyone who has sat in a classroom knows this is exactly how the best teachers keep their students on-track when conveying difficult concepts: establish an outline first, then add all the details, concepts, and analogies—but always in accordance with the original outline. This is how the best teachers teach, and it's exactly how God develops the truths in His Word. Master outline, details, sub-outlines, repeat.

If this principle was not in the DNA of God's prophetic Word, it would be impossible to connect the dots with any reliability. Confusion would reign...and God is not the author of confusion.

5. All the major details must be accounted for.

   o There's no such thing as partial credit when it comes to interpreting prophecy. The interpretation is either all right, or it's all wrong. The details are either all accounted for, or they're all suspect. That's because the Word of God is logical, accurate, and complete in all respects...and thus **the "lens" or "prism" through which a prophetic passage is interpreted must produce a scenario that's logical, accurate, and complete in all respects**, as well. If an expositor's lens (that is, his interpretive filter or starting point through which the details are analyzed) can explain four components of a prophecy, but not the fifth, then something is wrong with that lens. Likewise, if an expositor ignores a major clue, or if he stretches the interpretation of that clue just to make it "fit" his theory, then his scenario is inherently flawed. It must be reevaluated and, if necessary, discarded.

   This is not to disparage any expositor or his work. All current interpretations of prophecy—including mine—stand on the accumulated knowledge, research, and hypotheses of thousands of incredibly gifted scholars and pastors who've come before. The point is simply that we must judge a scenario based on its cohesiveness and ability to explain all the major details. Otherwise, we'll never arrive at the right conclusions.

6. It's not rocket science.

   o Inasmuch as Jesus commanded the humble churches in Asia Minor to study and decipher the prophecies of Revelation, we know that the correct interpretation of those prophecies must be relatively simple. **It shouldn't take a degree in theology or ancient history to explain the various symbols or to grasp their meaning**.

For instance, Jesus was able to explain *all* of the Old Testament prophecies which proved he was the Messiah in less than three hours, as he walked with two of his disciples on the road to Emmaus. (See Luke 24:13-35.)

Similarly, the people who made up the churches of Revelation were simple farmers, laborers, merchants, and craftsmen, not post-graduates of a theological seminary. (Although I'm very glad we have such seminaries!) The original seven congregations scattered around Asia Minor would have been familiar with the Roman emperors, their own national history, the local cults, and the Scriptures, but not much more.

Thus, any analysis that relies on novel translations of the text, or cleverly nuanced scenarios, or long-winded essays, is probably wrong. The text of the Bible is clear and concise, and therefore the explanation of prophecy should be clear and concise, as well. The prophet Daniel, for example, said the interpretation of his prophecies would occur as a function of *time* and a person's *faith in God's Word*, not as a function of academic IQ. (Specifically, Daniel said his prophecies would be understood in the *last days* by those who were *spiritually wise*.)

Thus, as we attempt to unlock the mysteries of Daniel and John, a good rule of thumb is to look for the simplest answer that can account for all the details, while still adhering to the biblical text. We shouldn't have to go very far to find the solution.

[Again, this is not to detract from the inestimable work of those who've given us the foundations of modern eschatology. It is simply a way to gauge the validity of *any* interpretation — including mine — by acknowledging the fact that deciphering prophecy should be a relatively straight-forward proposition. All one needs is a working knowledge of God's Word (II Tim. 2:15) and a genuine love for Christ (Jn. 16:13).]

7. Prophets look forward, not backward.

   o Each of the narratives recorded by Daniel and John begins in the time-frame that exists at the moment the prophecy is given. The narratives then proceed from that point into the future; they never look back. This is because prophecy, by its very nature, is not concerned with the past, but with what will happen in the future if people refuse to put away sin and turn to God. The only exception to this rule is when the narrative requires a set-up, and then only briefly.

   Thus, Daniel 2 and 7 start their narratives with Babylon, because the Babylonian kings were firmly in power when Daniel received those visions. Daniel 8 starts with a description of the Medo-Persian Empire, because the Medes were getting ready to supplant Babylon when that vision was given. Similarly, Revelation 12 begins with the activities of the Roman Empire, because that was the empire in power when John received the Apocalypse.

8. There will be exactly four prophetic empires in history.

   The prophet Daniel taught in verses 2:40 and 7:17 that from the sixth century B.C. until the establishment of God's kingdom on earth, exactly **four empires** would rise on the timeline of prophecy:

   Daniel 7:7 (GW) — Four kingdoms...will rise to power on the earth.

In Daniel 2 these four empires are represented by the **four components** of a statue that appeared in a dream to King Nebuchadnezzar of Babylon. They included: a head of gold, arms of silver, a belly and thighs of brass, and legs of iron. (The legs of iron represent phase one of the final empire; the feet of iron and clay represent phase two of the same empire.)

The four prophetic empires appear again in Daniel 7. But in this case they are represented by **four vicious animals**: a winged lion, a lopsided bear, a four-headed leopard, and a strange beast with ten horns. (The beast itself represents phase one of the final empire; the horns of the beast represent phase two.)

In the New Testament, this same "empire count" is repeated. It's reflected in the **four components** of a terrifying beast that appears in Revelation 13. The four components include: the body of a leopard, the feet of a bear, the mouth of a lion, and the beast as a whole.

Although the Bible never says why these four empires *in particular* are included on the list, one can make an educated guess. Apparently, it's because all of them share two unique characteristics.

First, each of these empires — and only these empires — subjugated the sovereign nation of Judaea. And second, each of these empires — and only these empires — directly threatened the line of Messiah by concentrating their forces on the tribe of Judah, the line through which Jesus was to come, thus threatening the entire plan of Salvation.

Consequently, as we go forward and attempt to explain the symbology of Daniel and the Apocalypse, we must stay within the framework of **exactly four empires** — not five, or seven, or eight, as some suggest.

9. In the Apocalypse, one symbol can represent several entities.

o Whereas the prophet Daniel uses several symbols to represent a single entity — for example, in referring to Greece he uses a torso of bronze (v. 2:32), a four-headed leopard (v. 7:6), and a goat with a large horn (v. 8:5) — **John the apostle reverses that formula and uses one symbol to represent several entities**.

For instance, in Revelation 12, the **Dragon** represents:

- The Antichrist spirit – Satan (Rev. 12:9)
- The Antichrist forces – An imperial army (Rev. 12:13-15)
- The Antichrist person – Seven kings (Rev. 12:3, 17:10)

In Revelation 13 and 17 the **Beast from the Sea** represents:

- The Antichrist spirit – Satan (Rev. 17:3)
- The Antichrist forces – An imperial army (Rev. 13:7)
- The Antichrist person – The Eighth King (Rev. 13:18)

In Revelation 17 the **Whore of Babylon** represents a certain city that is:

- A religious capital (Rev. 17:4-5, 16)
- An economic capital (Rev. 18)
- A political capital (Rev. 17:9-15)

Traditionally, expositors have tried to peg each of these symbols to a single entity. For example, many commentators insist the Whore of Babylon stands for the Vatican — and only the Vatican. Others believe that the Beast refers to the final kingdom — and nothing but the final kingdom.

However, such rigid interpretations inevitably fail once the remaining details of the prophecy are applied. (For example, one look at Revelation 18 tells us the Whore of Babylon, in addition to being a religious capital, also serves as the capital of a global economic empire.) Therefore, interpreting the symbols on a "single-entity" basis is a faulty method of interpretation because it produces a slew of contradictions and disagreements.

On the other hand, if we simply acknowledge that, in the book of Revelation, each symbol or "creature" has two or three different aspects, and allow the context to tell us *which* aspect is in view, then all the "contradictions" surrounding the identification of these symbols are instantly resolved. Our interpretations suddenly become logical and consistent.[65]

10. The Bible uses the following imagery to symbolize kings, kingdoms, wicked cities, and Satan. It thus might be helpful to keep these icons in mind as we go through the relevant prophecies:

o **Beast** – A godless king, his kingdom, or Satan
    [Gen. 3:1; Is. 27:1; Dan. 7:3-26; Rev. 12:3, 13:1, 11]

o **Horn** – An evil king, the military power of that king, or the nation(s) he commands
    [Ezek. 29:21; Dan. 7:24, 8:20; Rev. 17:12]

---

[65] The 3-in-1 concept is not foreign to Scripture. For example, the Bible clearly teaches there is only one God, but when the word "God" appears in a passage, that passage could be speaking about God the Father (e.g., Is. 63:16; Mt. 3:17), God the Holy Spirit (e.g., Ex. 35:31; Lk. 3:22), or God the Son (e.g., Pr. 2:12, Jn. 20:28). Context determines which one is in view. Similarly, the Apocalypse often uses one symbol to represent three closely related entities or aspects thereof. Our job is to determine which entity or aspect is in view, based on the context and a bit of common sense.

o **Harlot** – A city or nation drenched in false religion
  [Jer. 3:6; Is. 1:21; Nahum 3:4; Is. 23:15; Rev. 17:5]

o **Tree:**

  – Israel
  [Mt. 24:32 (the "fig tree"); Judges 9:7-15 ("the trees"); Mk. 11:13, 20 (the "fig tree"); 2 Kings 19:23 (the "tall cedar trees")]

  – The Gentile nations
  [Lk. 21:29 ("all the trees"); Rom. 11:16-27 (the "branches")]

  – Christ
  [Jer. 17:8; Job 14:7; Ps. 52:8; Hos. 14:5-8; Is. 11:1]

  – Antichrist Type
  [Dan. 4:10-12 (Nebuchadnezzar); Judges 9:14-15 (Abimelech); Ezek. 31:3-14 (Asnapper the "Assyrian")]

APPENDIX B

SAMPLE OF PASTORS, WEBSITES, and AUTHORS WHO SAY THE ANTICHRIST WILL BE (OR IS LIKELY TO BE) ISLAMIC

A Matter of Truth - YouTube channel

Armageddon News - YouTube channel

Jimmy Evans - Pastor, Gateway Church

Phillip Goodman - Author, *The Assyrian Connection*

James Graziano - Pastor, The Faith Tabernacle

John Hagee - Pastor, Cornerstone Church

Jerel Hagerman - Pastor, Joshua Springs Calvary Church

Bob Hunt - Zion's Hope Ministry

John MacArthur - Pastor, Grace Community Church

Joel Richardson - Author, Speaker, and Filmmaker

Gary Shiohama - Pastor, South Bay Community Church

Walid Shoebat - Author, *God's War on Terror*

Perry Stone - Pastor, Voice of Evangelism Ministries

Jack Van Koevering - Author, *The Man of Sin*

Michael Youssef - Pastor, The Church of the Apostles

And many others…

[CONTINUED]

On the other hand, many prophecy teachers still support the **Roman Antichrist** position, a viewpoint with which I agree. These include such notable pastors and authors as:

Jimmy DeYoung

Daymond Duck

Jack Hibbs

Ed Hindson

Mark Hitchcock

Thomas Ice

Jerry Jenkins

Hal Lindsey

Jan Markell

Donald Perkins

Dave Reagan

Ron Rhodes

And many others…

APPENDIX C

PASTOR JOHN MACARTHUR'S STATEMENT REGARDING THE ISLAMIC ORIGIN OF THE ANTICHRIST

Transcript of a YouTube video entitled "The Mahdi is the Antichrist – John MacArthur" [time mark = 19:27 - 21:25]

Now somebody might say, "Well, you know, when you think about the future and what's going to happen in the world, don't we have a revived Roman Empire? Doesn't that mean the West?"

You'll remember that the image in Daniel 2, of the final world empire, had two legs. And the Roman Empire had the West [half] and the East [half]. You know, of course, if you know history, that the Western part of the Roman Empire basically dissolved, and the East survived for a thousand years or more, so that (at the time of the New Testament) sixty-percent of the Roman Empire was land that is now under Muslim control. At least sixty-percent. The vast majority of the Roman Empire in New Testament times is today under Muslim control. And Islam is moving across the West rapidly in Europe, isn't it?

When you have a picture in Ezekiel 38, you have a picture of the Antichrist, "Gog," and you have the listing of eight nations that will be a coalition for the Antichrist. All eight of those are Muslim nations—all eight of them! And they ring the Mediterranean all the way to Libya.

In Revelation 17:9–11 it says there were six kingdoms, and then a seventh, and finally an eighth. What is the seventh? Well, there's been discussion about that. It well could be the Ottoman Turk Empire which lasted 500 years and didn't really fall until the modern era. The Turkish empire was the last caliphate, which ended in 1923. And they're waiting for the restoration when the Mahdi comes.

Pastor MacArthur is an honorable man and a very good teacher. And I have no doubt he would deny that he bases his theory of a Muslim Antichrist on Islamic eschatology. But the impression he leaves on his audience (intended or not) is that Muslim eschatology — especially the "parallels" between the Mahdi and the Antichrist — reinforces something that is already taught in Scripture, namely, that the Antichrist will be a Muslim, and that the "Eighth Kingdom" will be a new Islamic caliphate—or maybe even the reincarnation of an old caliphate, such as the mighty Ottoman Empire.

Perhaps a better approach for this sermon would've been to simply stick to the scriptures which "prove" the Antichrist will be a Muslim, and then, as an aside, observe that at least 1.4 billion Muslims will readily embrace the Antichrist as their savior because he will appear to be the individual they've been expecting.

But, either way, it is clear that Pastor MacArthur agrees with the theory that the Antichrist will come out of Islam, and that theory is all I'm trying to disprove in this essay.

APPENDIX D

BLOODLINE OF THE ANTICHRIST

As I stated in *The Challenge!* on page 7, Abraham was anointed by God to *bless* the nations by producing Jesus Christ, not *curse* the nations by producing the Antichrist. It is therefore impossible for the Antichrist to descend from Abraham, which means he cannot be an Arab, which means he cannot be the so-called *Mahdi*.

But if the Antichrist cannot descend from Abraham, then from whom will he come? Who were his forefathers?

In my opinion, the Antichrist will descend from the tribes of Magog, Meshech, and Tubal. And I believe that axiom because the prophet Ezekiel all but stated it in chapter 38 of his book. Ezekiel calls the Antichrist by his title, "Gog" (i.e., most high), and says in verse 2:

> Son of man, set thy face against
> Gog [of] the land of **Magog** ...
> [Gog] the chief prince of **Meshech** and **Tubal**,
> and prophesy against him.

Here, Ezekiel is actually addressing two separate "Gogs."

Gog 1 is "Gog of the land of Magog." This was the warrior-king who reigned just before the time of Ezekiel and raided neighboring territories from his base in Lydia.[66] (The region of Lydia had been inhabited by Gog's kinsmen—the tribes of Magog, Meshech, and Tubal—ever since their dispersal from the Tower of Babel. It lies to the northwest of Israel and is now part of western Turkey.)[67]

---

66 See article by Jeffrey Goodman, Ph. D. ▶ http://www.newscientificevidenceforgod.com/2012/02/debunking-russiawar-of-gog-and-magog.html

67 See: IVP Atlas of Bible History, New Moody Atlas of the Bible, Holman Bible Atlas, Zondervan Atlas of the Bible, ESV Atlas, Harper-Collins Atlas of Bible History, etc.

This was the man whom the Lord told Ezekiel to face as he prophesied about the last days. And part of the reason Ezekiel was told to face *that* "Gog" is because his distant *grandson*, **Gog 2** — a.k.a., "Gog the chief prince of Meshech and Tubal" — is really the Antichrist.

Yes. I realize that claiming **Gog 2** is really the Antichrist might rankle some prophecy experts. But I believe it is true because Ezekiel says **Gog 2** will participate in the Battle of Armageddon (v. 38:7-9), *and* he will be defeated in-person by the Lord himself (v. 38:20), a fate not ascribed to anyone but the Antichrist.[68]

The question, of course, is this:

> If—as I have repeatedly stated—the Antichrist is a *Roman Caesar* who will rise out of Italy, then how can he be the *Chief Prince of Meshech and Tubal* at the same time? How is that even possible?

The answer is simple: it is because the Antichrist is *both*. He is both the Chief Prince of Meshech and Tubal *and* a Roman Caesar.

You see, after studying this issue at length, I'm convinced the people of Rome sprang not only from the clans who originally settled the Italian peninsula after the Flood, but also from the tribes of Magog, Meshech, and Tubal, some of whose members *undoubtedly* migrated westward by land or by sea (or both) to the very same peninsula over the course of time.[69] (Please see map on the next page.)

And thus, the Roman kings, followed by the Roman Caesars, and now the final Caesar—the Antichrist—trace their lineage not only to the people who initially populated Italy after the Flood, but also to the

---

[68] See the article, "Six Reasons Why Gog is the Antichrist," at www.joelstrumpet.com

[69] Although the testimony of archaeology and DNA is not yet sufficient to draw scientific conclusions about the origin of the Roman people (for example, see Wikipedia: "Etruscan origins"), no one who believes in the authority of God's Word can doubt that, based on sheer logic, the natural migration pattern from the Tower of Babel would have eventually brought some of the people of Lydia (now western Turkey) to Italy, whether by land, or sea, or both.

tribes of *Magog, Meshech, and Tubal*, some of whose members arrived several centuries later.

Consequently, since the Antichrist is the ultimate descendant of **Gog 1** and his kinsmen (**Magog, Meshech, and Tubal**) then he—even as the final Caesar of Rome—is properly called:

- Gog (i.e., Gog 2)

- Chief (ultimate)

- Prince of (ruler from)

- Meshech and Tubal (the original tribes)

The following charts might help to clarify my position. They portray the migration pattern and genealogy of the Antichrist bloodline, according to my understanding of the relevant passages:

MIGRATION PATTERN OF THE ANTICHRIST BLOODLINE

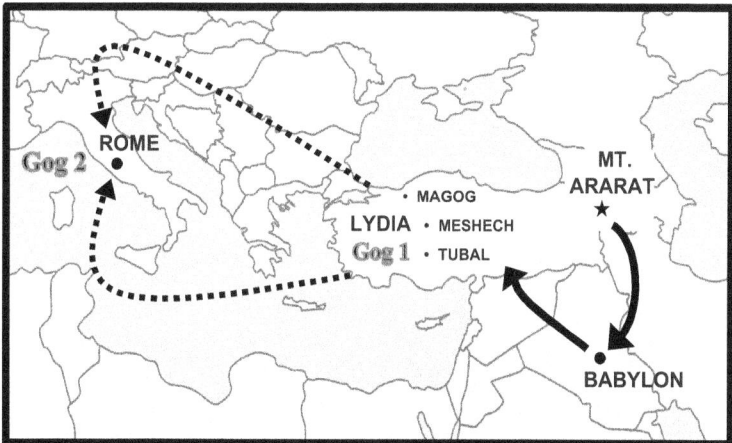

Hence, just as Luke traced the lineage of Jesus from Adam to Abraham to Joseph, so too does Ezekiel trace the lineage of the Antichrist from Japheth to the tribes of Lydia, to Gog 1, and then Rome.

Lineage of the Roman Antichrist

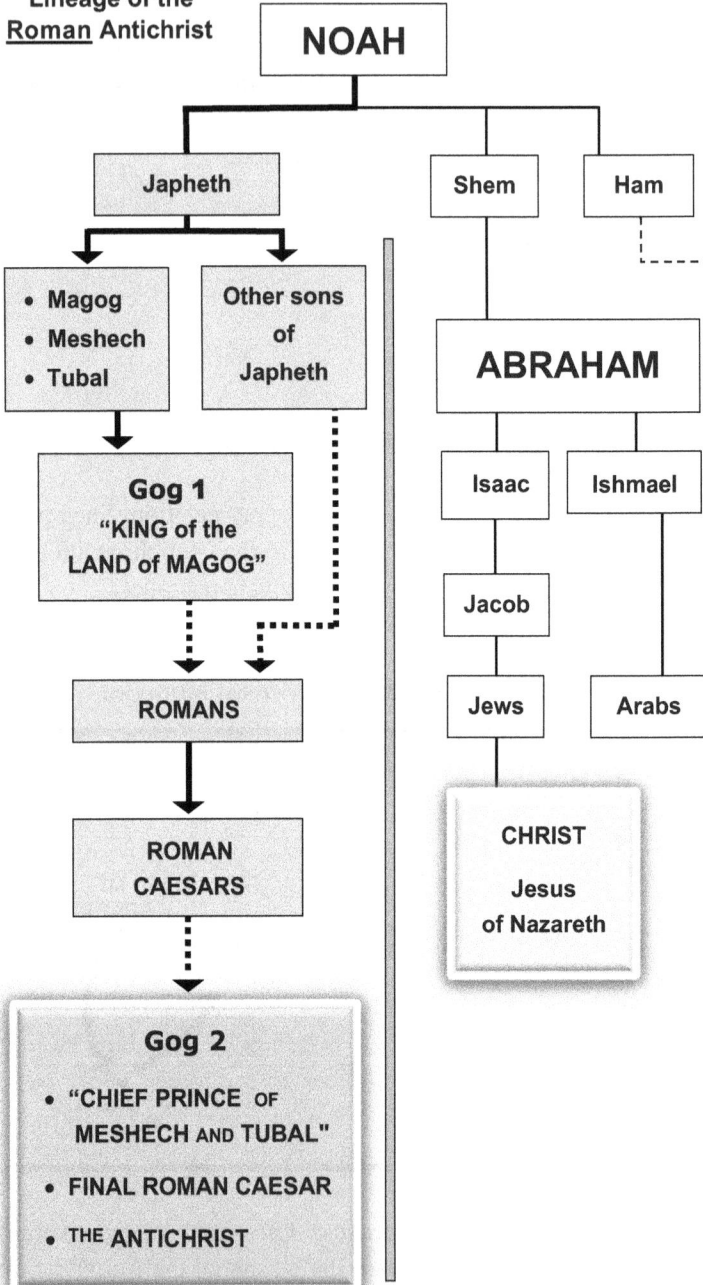

NOAH

- **Japheth**
  - Magog
  - Meshech
  - Tubal
  - Other sons of Japheth

  Gog 1
  "KING of the LAND of MAGOG"

  ROMANS

  ROMAN CAESARS

  Gog 2
  - "CHIEF PRINCE OF MESHECH AND TUBAL"
  - FINAL ROMAN CAESAR
  - THE ANTICHRIST

- **Shem**

  ABRAHAM
  - Isaac
    - Jacob
      - Jews

        CHRIST
        Jesus of Nazareth
  - Ishmael
    - Arabs

- **Ham**

* * * * *

Dear Reader,

If you enjoyed this book, it would mean a lot to this author if you could leave a short review on Amazon or on any of your favorite bookstore websites. Your input would help me fine tune my upcoming essays, and it would give other last days enthusiasts a chance to gauge the quality of these works up front.

Thank you for taking an interest in Bible prophecy and for giving me an opportunity to share some of my thoughts and insights with you. Writing this book has been a blessing to me, and I hope that reading *The Islamic Antichrist Myth* has been a blessing to you, as well!

Sincerely,

Charles "Ken" Bassett

* * * * *

ADDITIONAL POSITRON BOOKS

God Says Count the Number 666! Why the Church Can Discover the Identity of the Antichrist! (2020)

- Has Satan been grooming an Antichrist candidate in each generation?
- Is the 666 code meant for post-Rapture believers…or the Church?
- How does God use prophecy to save people from judgment?
- Does "imminence" prevent the Church from discovering the Beast?
- Which verse says the Antichrist can't be identified till after the Rapture? (Hint: There is none!)

Empire of the Antichrist (2020)

- Will the Antichrist come from America, Arabia, Turkey, or Rome?
- Where is the first prophecy recorded in Scripture?
- Which empire of history is the last empire of prophecy?
- Who are the Beast, the Seven Heads, and the Ten Horns?
- Who—or what—is the Whore of Babylon?
- Which verse controls the order and content of Daniel and Revelation?

The Islamic Antichrist Myth (2020)

- Where is "Satan's throne" located
- How can an Islamic leader claim to be God?
- Will Muslims actually worship the Antichrist?
- Will the Antichrist conquer the previous empires of prophecy?
- Is the Beast of Revelation an Arab, a Persian, a Turk…or an Italian?

Coming soon...

The Whore of Babylon (2021)

- Is she a country, a religion, an economic empire...or an ancient city?
- Why was John scolded for being "amazed" at her appearance?
- What does her title "Babylon the Great" really mean?
- Why will the Antichrist and his cohorts destroy her?
- How can she "sit" on the Beast?

Gog of Magog (2021)

- Is Gog a Russian strongman...or the Roman Antichrist?
- Will Gog's War take place when the Tribulation begins...or ends?
- Is Gog's War really just another name for Armageddon?
- Can we construct a Tribulation timeline, based on Scripture?
- Is the Whore of Babylon punished once...or twice?

The False Prophet (2021)

- Is the False Prophet a Jew or a Gentile?
- Was he born before, during, or after 1948?
- Why does the False Prophet have two horns like a lamb?
- Is the False Prophet admired and respected by Christians today?
- What does the Bible mean when it says he will "speak like a dragon"?

The Antichrist (2021)

- Where will the Antichrist come from? Is he alive today?
- Is he a master of the occult? What does the 666 code mean?
- Is he a homosexual…or is he married with children?
- Is he a Secular Humanist, a Jew, or a Muslim?
- Is he the biological offspring of Satan?

What Every Christian Should Know (2021)

Believe it or not, a recent survey shows that most Christians have trouble correctly defining the Gospel. Many are unable to properly state what it takes for a person to be saved. And only a handful can list the Ten Commandments. So imagine having a small pamphlet that can boost one's knowledge of Christian fundamentals, and provide the necessary foundation upon which to lead others to Christ. Brief and to the point, this book clears up many misconceptions and enables believers to "know what they believe." Great for new Christians!

How to Witness Like Jesus and the Apostles (2021)

Would you be surprised to learn that Jesus *never* said:

- You should thoroughly befriend people before witnessing to them.
- There's a God-shaped hole in your heart that only the Lord can fill.
- God has a wonderful plan for your life.
- God is not angry with sinners.

Learn how Jesus *actually* presented the Gospel to others. No one did it better!

Darwin's Apocalypse (2021)

- Why do so many biologists privately admit that Evolution is false?
- How many laws of nature does the theory of Evolution violate?
- Do programs like AVIDA prove Evolution is true...or just the opposite?
- Has anyone ever seen Evolution produce a new kind of animal?
- Why is the following equation fatally flawed:

$$(\text{Random Mutation} \times \text{Natural Selection})^n = \text{New Species}$$

Please visit Prophecy7000.com for updates!

ABOUT THE AUTHOR

Charles "Ken" Bassett has enjoyed the study of prophecy ever since a friend handed him a copy of Hal Lindsey's *The Late, Great Planet Earth* in 1978. Shortly after that pivotal moment, Charles gave his life to Christ and began searching the Scriptures to see what God says about such topics as the Rapture, the Tribulation, the Antichrist, and the glorious return of Jesus.

Realizing that a wealth of end-time information and insight also exists in the writings of incredibly gifted scholars, pastors, and expositors, Charles began devouring their works, as well.

Now, after a lifetime of study, Charles has put forth his own observations on such topics as the Beast, the False Prophet, and the Whore of Babylon.

In his latest work, *The Islamic Antichrist Myth*, Charles dispels one of the most popular end-time theories to emerge in recent years, namely, that the Antichrist will be a Muslim. While this new theory may be popular, he says, it is not supported by Scripture, and could cause the Church to miss key events and personalities related to the imminent return of Christ.

Moreover, this conjecture seems to be driven more by the drama of current international events and a willingness to reference Islamic prophecy, than by solid exegesis. Not surprisingly, says Charles, the Islamic Antichrist Theory contains at least fifteen serious errors. And it is those errors which Charles exposes and corrects in *The Islamic Antichrist Myth*.

On a more personal note, Charles now lives near Austin, Texas, with his college sweetheart and wife of forty years, Denise. They have five grown children and seven grandchildren. Charles was a T-37 instructor pilot and a C-141 airlift pilot with the Air Force during the 1980s. Afterwards, he was hired by a major airline, where he still enjoys flying international routes as a B-777 captain.

In addition to *The Islamic Antichrist Myth*, and other related titles, Charles has also published a children's book, *Timmy and His Flying Saucer*, through Christian Faith Publishing.

www.ingramcontent.com/pod-product-compliance
Lightning Source LLC
Chambersburg PA
CBHW072014040426
42447CB00009B/1634